The Royal British Legion

...and one small branch in Devon

by
Paddy King-Fretts

List of contents

Acknowledgement

The author is indebted to Brigadier Brian Harding CBE, MC for kindly allowing him access to his book *'Keeping Faith'*, the history of the Royal British Legion, and for permitting him to use a number of his photographs. In addition he would like to thank Haig House for their support throughout this project and for their financial assistance in bringing the book to publication. And finally he would like to thank Barry Price for the countless hours he spent pouring over the text and for his invaluable criticism and advice.

Foreword

This is a very special little book. It punches way above it's weight and tells us much. A short history of the Royal British Legion - about which most of us know little - is explained simply and clearly. We read about success and achievement down the years, trials and tribulations in war and peace. We learn of the problems confronting the RBL and what it must do to survive in its present form.

However, and for me this is the best part, we read about how South Molton, one small branch in Devon, has succeeded, and succeeded so admirably. No doubt a team effort, their success has been achieved by the members themselves. And what a team! No less that sixty-five of them have written of their experiences that range from the horrors of World War II, right up to the current operations in Afghanistan. Fascinating stories indeed that tell us much about our country's servicemen and women. They served their Sovereign and their Country with pride and fortitude. They asked for nothing yet gave much. It is a marvellous read which I enjoyed enormously and which I strongly recommend.

Simon Weston OBE
Falkland's veteran

Sir Hugh Stucley Bt. DL.,
Affeton Castle,
East Worlington,
Crediton,
Devon EX17 4TU

Introduction
by Sir Hugh Stucley Bt DL,
President of the South Molton Branch of the RBL

I suspect that, until recently, I was like most other people in that I knew precious little about the Royal British Legion. To so many, it is a charity that appears but once a year, in November, when it sells us our poppies and leads us in remembering the fallen. But there is so much more to the organisation that we really should know about - and which this little book tells us.

The basic aims of the RBL, as set out in their charter, are well covered by the authors early on. But it is surely down at grass roots level - in the clubs and branches up and down the country - that the organisation will stand or fall. The book will tell you how one small branch in North Devon, of which I am privileged to be President, has achieved such wonders. South Molton is but a small market town on the edge of Exmoor, yet the RBL here is in tremendous form - the last Chairman being awarded the MBE for services to the Legion, in winning a prestigious national RBL competition, by being awarded a county trophy and, finally, by being honoured to receive a letter of acknowledgement from The Queen. And it is the members of the Branch themselves who have made all this happen. You will meet them here - of all ages, all ranks and from all three Services.

Between them they have served their Sovereign and their country in every theatre from Dunkirk to Afghanistan, from the Arctic to Arabia, and from the Falklands to Iraq. Several are still serving today, and all of them are proud, yet unassuming, at what they have together achieved. It is through members such as these that branches will flourish, and it is from branches and clubs like South Molton that the RBL draws such strength.

As you read the tales our members tell, one thing above all else will be going through your mind, and that is 'Serving their Country'. I am proud of what they have achieved and, I'm sure, you will be proud of them too.

Hugh Stucley

A short history of The Royal British Legion

In the Beginning

The guns finally fell silent on 11th November 1918, but it was to be three long years before The British Legion, as it was originally known, came into being. Only then was Earl Haig able to announce the formation of the charity. In the intervening time, Great Britain, like most other European nations, took stock: all but paralysed by the appalling cost of the Great War. In manpower alone Great Britain and Ireland lost 885,000 dead – an almost unbelievable figure of 570 for each and every day of that terrible conflict. Furthermore there were between three and four times that number of wounded – somewhere between two and a half and three million. A generation had been virtually annihilated: every family in the land had been touched. The welfare and medical services, such as existed then, were simply overwhelmed. Add to all this the fact that the population back in 1918 was barely half what it is today and the true magnitude of the agony becomes apparent.

Very slowly the country emerged from its dazed and broken state, and began to feel its way ahead. In their own tragic way the war dead were the least of the problems confronting the nation. They had gone for ever and there was nothing anybody could do except collect them together, bury them with dignity and vow to remember them. The principal concern facing the nation was the wounded. The steady stream of casualties which, only too frequently, rose to a torrent, bore down heavily. Long before the war was over a number of organizations came into being in an attempt to help the multitude of wounded veterans. It must be remembered that, back then, the hospitals were few and far between, there was no NHS, no welfare state or other benefits, and no charitable organizations that could cope. Those in trouble were, quite literally, on their own. Either they struggled on and survived, or else they fell by the wayside.

In 1916 (the year of the Somme) 'The National Association of Discharged Sailors and Soldiers' was founded in Blackburn with strong links to the Trade Unions and their political arm – the Labour party. The following year (Ypres and Passendale), 'The National Federation of Discharged and Demobilized Sailors and Soldiers' came into being. Founded in London and with branches throughout the South East, this charity had strong connections to the Liberal Party. By the end of this year, yet a third organization had been created: 'Comrades of The Great War'. It was non-political, having instead at its head such national figures as the Duke of Westminster and Lords Rothermere and Northcliffe, with Captain Towse VC as its Chairman. After the war the humanitarian problems were exacerbated further when millions of servicemen returned to a stunned and destitute country that had no jobs for them, and little to offer in the way of help. This situation thus spawned a fourth organization. 'The National Union of Ex-servicemen' . Born out of the post-war turbulence and strongly left wing, it was more radical than the others and preyed on the dissatisfaction of those coming home.

Here then were four separate organizations all striving to help those in need, sometimes working together but more often finding themselves in competition or conflict with each other. The result was a hopeless muddle that failed to get on top of the enormous problems associated with dealing with the afflicted. Something had to be done. The following year saw efforts to merge one or other of these organizations, but it was not until towards the end of 1920 that any serious advances were made. Success came finally on Saturday 14th May 1921 (Whitsun weekend) when over seven hundred delegates met in London. The Prince of Wales (then a revered figure) was elected as Patron, with Earl Haig (by now a National hero) being voted in as President by 658 votes to 49. It should be noted that, at this time, both men were immensely popular nationwide, and both threw themselves wholeheartedly behind the cause.

The men who created the Legion: Field Marshal Earl Haig and Mr T.F.Lister

Elected as Chairman of this new organization was a remarkable character, a Mr Tom Lister (later Sir Frederick Lister). Hailing from a more modest background, he served in the ranks until wounded and discharged in 1916, and was, by this time, Chairman of the Federation. His genius was in taking the chair and this he did forcefully, dominating the early and somewhat fraught meetings until a satisfactory state of affairs had been reached. He remained Chairman until shortly before Earl Haig's death in 1928 and is widely regarded as having been the power behind getting the Legion off the ground, and steering the way through those first difficult years. The name of the new body was decided at the first Unity Committee meeting on 30th June 1921. No less than forty-nine suggestions were put forward including such propositions as 'Warriors' Guild' and 'Imperial Federation of Comrades', but the Federation's suggestion of 'British Legion' carried the day. The basic purpose of the British Legion was straightforward enough, namely to care for those who had suffered as a result of service during the Great War. Although the wording of the charter has changed several times down the years, the basic tenets have remained much the same.

In essence they are:

> To remember the fallen.
> To be the voice of the afflicted.
> To raise money in order to help those in need.
> To provide a focal point for those seeking help or comradeship.

It is perhaps now time to take a brief look at how the various ideas for Remembrance first came about, then how they came together to form our ceremonies we know today.

The Poppy

The concept of having the poppy as a symbol of remembrance came early in the war. In 1915 a Canadian doctor, Colonel John McCrae, realized that the only thing which appeared to survive on the battlefield was the poppy. Through a combination of the ingredients of high explosive charges and the chalky soil of Flanders, or simply where the soil had been disturbed, the poppy survived almost alone, and the sight of these beautiful flowers carpeting the desolation inspired him to write his famous poem 'In Flanders' Fields', the first verse of which runs thus:

> In Flanders' fields the poppies blow
> Between the crosses row on row,
> That mark our place: and in the sky
> The larks, still bravely singing, fly
> Scarce heard amid the guns below.

And concludes:

> If ye break faith with us who die
> We shall not sleep, though poppies grow
> In Flanders' fields.

But it was not until 1918 that an American War Secretary, Moina Michael, bought twenty-five poppies from a department store and sold them in an attempt to raise funds. Her initial effort was an astonishing success and year after year every poppy she and her friends made was sold. Three years later the fledgling British Legion took up her idea and held its first National Poppy Day on 11th November 1921. Here, too, the poppy struck an immediate chord with the public when the nine million offered for sale ran out. The trick now would be to get enough poppies made for the following year. And it was here that a Major George Howson, MC stepped forward. With funds from the Legion he set up a poppy factory just off the Old Kent Road. Staffed by disabled ex-servicemen, their order for the following year was for a massive thirty million. Again the effort was a success, thus the decision to manufacture the poppies in the UK was well justified. Years later the factory moved to a new site at Richmond where it remains today and where, no sooner has one Remembrance Sunday passed, work begins for the following year.

The Exhortation

The 1929 Remembrance Festival was held for the first time in London's Albert Hall when, to a packed and emotional house, the massed standards of the branches of the Legion were carried on to the platform. It was at this moment that the words of another famous poem were used as an exhortation to those present to remember those who had fallen.

Laurence Binyon was over forty at the outbreak of the war and, time and again, he was rejected as being too old for the fight. A scholar and Keeper of the Oriental Prints at the British Museum, and one blessed with acute premonition, he penned the immortal words of his poem 'To the Fallen' while on holiday in Cornwall soon after the outbreak of war. Later his insistence on serving his country was finally acknowledged and he found himself posted as a lowly porter to a Field Hospital behind the front lines in Normandy. It was here that he witnessed the full horrors of war where the dead, the wounded and the dying were brought back to the hospital in a continuous stream. When casualties were particularly heavy, or immediately prior to an offensive, he and others had to push the corpses, still unburied and already putrefying, to one side in order to make room for fresh casualties. It was, he later remarked, as though the dead had simply been forgotten. Thus it was from this grim scenario, that his earlier prescience proved to have been so perceptive. The Legion took the fourth verse of his poem.

> They shall grow not old as we that are left grow old.
> Age shall not weary them nor the years condemn.
> At the going down of the sun and in the morning
> We will remember them.

Throughout the Legion these words became known as the 'Exhortation' and the following year the National Executive Council decreed that they were to be spoken at the beginning of every Council meeting. The practice spread throughout the country so that the words became the preamble to any formal meeting, be it at national level or down at grass roots whenever branches or clubs met. It is a tradition that is carried on to this day.

The Cenotaph

The War Memorial in Whitehall, The Cenotaph (a monument to those buried elsewhere), began life as a temporary structure built out of wood and plaster, erected as the focal point for the London Victory Parade on 19th July 1919. However, such was the outpouring of national sentiment that a few days later the Prime Minister, David Lloyd George, summoned the architect, Sir Edwin Lutyens, and proposed that a permanent memorial should be erected on the same spot, and that it should be known as Britain's official national war memorial. This was built from Portland stone between 1919 and 1920, the architects waiving their fee of £7,300 (almost £400k today) on completion.

The new memorial was unveiled by King George V on 11th November 1920, the second anniversary of the Armistice with Germany. This particular ceremony was part of a larger procession bringing home the Unknown British Warrior to be laid to rest in Westminster Abbey. As the funeral procession passed the Cenotaph, the cortege paused to allow the waiting King to lay a wreath on the Unknown Warrior's gun-carriage. The Cenotaph having been unveiled already, the monarch then joined the procession on its way to Westminster Abbey. Years later, in the Summer of 1946, the Cenotaph was rededicated to include those who had fallen in World War II. Today the monument commemorates all those who have fallen in war.

While London remains the nation's focal point, where the Royal Family and Government gather together with thousands of Legionnaires to pay their respects, it is out in the towns, the cities and the small villages that the nation pays more personal tributes. Here the local men and women salute their fallen, and here the wives and widows, the daughters and sons grieve. For it is here, across the nation, that lies the heart of the Legion. Throughout the country, Legion branches, large and small, lead the people in remembering those who did not come home. It has been that way ever since.

The Tomb of the Unknown Warrior, Westminster Abbey

The idea for such a tomb appears to have originated from an Army Chaplain, the Reverend David Railton, back in 1916 when he came across a grave with a rough cross on which were penciled the words 'An Unknown British Soldier'. After the war he wrote to the Dean of Westminster through whose energies the memorial was carried into effect. It is interesting to note just how this particular warrior was selected for immortality.

The body came from a small number that had been exhumed from the battlefields of the Aisne, the Somme, Arras and Ypres. The remains were brought to the chapel at St Pol (now part of Dunkirk) on the night of 7th November. Here a Brigadier Wyatt and a blindfolded Colonel Gell went alone into the chapel where the bodies lay covered by Union Flags. They knew nothing about those lying there and had no idea from whence they came. After a short respectful pause, the Colonel reached out and touched one, which was placed in a plain coffin. The following day, and after a service had been held locally, the body was removed to Boulogne. Here the coffin was placed inside another made from two-inch thick English oak from Hampton Court, and zinc lined. Within the wrought iron bands of this second coffin was placed an ancient crusader's sword, selected by the King and brought from the Tower of London. On the coffin lid was the inscription, 'A British Warrior who fell in the Great War 1914-1918 for King and Country'.

Now draped with the Union Flag that Padre Railton had used as an altar cloth during his time at The Front, the coffin, carried to Dover by *HMS Verdun* and escorted by six battleships, then moved by train to Victoria Station. On the morning of 11th November the Unknown Warrior was placed on a gun carriage drawn by six black horses (war veterans themselves) to begin its final journey and, as mentioned earlier, paused briefly on the way at the Cenotaph where King George V placed his wreath of red roses and bay leaves. Now escorted by the monarch and the heads of the Armed Services, it made its way to the Abbey where it passed through a Guard of Honour made up of one hundred holders of the Victoria Cross. The guests of honour were a group of around one hundred women who had lost their husbands and all their sons in the war. As the Warrior was being lowered into his final resting place, the King stepped forward and scattered a handful of French soil onto the coffin.

The body of the Unknown Warrior may have come from any of the three services, Army, Navy or Air Force and represents all those who died in the conflict and who have no other memorial or known grave. In 1923, as Lady Elizabeth Bowes Lyon was leaving the Abbey after marrying the Duke of York, later King George VI, she laid her wedding bouquet on the grave as a spontaneous mark of respect (she had lost a brother during the war). All royal brides married in the Abbey since then have likewise laid their bouquets. The latest to do so was Miss Katherine Middleton after becoming the Duchess of Cambridge on marrying Prince William.

The long road ahead

All the essential ingredients were now in place for the British Legion to get on with its work. It seemed straight forward enough for such was the enthusiasm of both the National Council and branch members. However, the country remained in a dreadful state. Almost at once the Legion remonstrated with the Government over ex-Servicemen's pensions and other matters. But the coffers were empty and there were many other calls on the Government's time and money. Yet the Legion persisted. Some victories were hard won such as the 'Employment Preferences Act' and 'Maintaining War Pensions', but there were failures too – such as the setting up of a 'National Work Scheme', and the 'Right to Appeal against the Settlement of a Disability Pension' among others.

Then, in 1926, came the General Strike. Times had been hard enough but life now was to become harder still. There the Legion found itself in a quandary. Although non-political it had always been fiercely loyal to the Government. But now, and in particular among the mining and industrial areas of the Midlands and the North, branch members could see how their neighbourhoods were being affected by the strike. The conscience of members was torn: should they help the Government or should they look after the strikers? Mercifully the strike was short lived and the Legion, through skillful manoeuvring, managed to steer clear of controversy. It decided to remain out of the argument but to help those who were suffering by setting up soup kitchens, distributing food, and by running concerts and social events in order to raise money for those affected.

Hardly had the country got through the General Strike before it found itself in the grip of the Great Depression. Difficult times again, this time through the loss of jobs, for many Legionnaires were by now in their mid or late thirties, and were the family breadwinners. Once again the Legion rallied and in the early thirties was able to boast one of its all time greatest successes by finding jobs for many tens of thousands of their members and for helping families in distress. On the other hand many awkward hurdles had to be cleared such as the antagonism towards the Legion shown in Dublin and, at home, by the temporary emergence of the Peace Pledge Union with their white poppies: a movement that claimed indifferent support and which was short lived.

Further afield a far more sinister threat was emerging in the shape of Hitler's Nazi Germany. Once again the Legion found itself in an anomalous position. While working for peace through its contacts with similar organizations in other countries, it was nonetheless seen by others, through its militaristic style of banners and parades, and by its commemoration of the dead, as an institution that glorified war. However, the Legion's pursuit of peace prevailed to such an extent that the organization stretched its national credibility to the limit by making a direct appeal to Hitler himself. The idea, although not initiated by the Legion's Patron, was nonetheless endorsed fully by the Prince of Wales. In the event a small party led by the Chairman visited Berlin in July 1935.

The British Legion delegation meets Hitler at the Reichschancellerie. Berlin, July 1935

The visit was, of course, cleverly orchestrated by the Nazis, who laid on a tumultuous reception with maximum publicity. After a meeting with Hitler they were, quite astonishingly, taken to Dachau concentration camp where they witnessed the incarceration of political prisoners, before ending their day with a dinner party hosted by Himmler! The aim of the visit was that there should be no war between Great Britain and Germany. Having listened to the assurances of Hitler and others, the party appeared convinced and returned home in the belief that they had achieved their aim.

A reciprocal visit was arranged whereby the German delegation, dressed in their brown shirts, laid a wreath at the Cenotaph and gave the Nazi salute. Later the delegation was entertained to dinner at The Army and Navy Club in Pall Mall. However extraordinary and naïve these visits may now seem, they are nevertheless judged in hindsight. They took place several years before war broke out. Nobody knew what was going to happen next and one should not thus be too critical of the Legion's worthy intentions. However, later in 1937, a second visit to Germany took place when more meetings were held with the Nazi hierarchy. Again the visitors came away seemingly satisfied that all would be well. But by this time European affairs had deteriorated from bad to worse and there is little doubt that the British delegation should have been more circumspect, and shown a greater awareness of what was going on around them.

The Women's Section

In parallel with the formation of the British Legion itself there was, even in the earliest days, a strong move towards forming a Women's Section. Although few, if any, women had gone right up to 'The Front' during the war, millions of others were involved from positions just behind the front line, all the way back to war-employment at home. That said, nurses and ambulance drivers often found themselves within range of the guns, their efforts and the risks they took being widely appreciated by all who came across them. In depots and staging posts along the line women undertook all manner of administrative and welfare work, while 'back home' they worked in the cities, the factories and on the land, taking the places of men who had been called to the war. It was a remarkable demonstration of loyalty and equality, seeing that they were to be denied the same voting rights as men until 1928.

Once the war was over, ex-service women in some areas, but not all, were invited to join the Legion as it then stood. Regrettably old prejudices all too often prevailed and many of them found a less than welcoming atmosphere in their local branches. Those who had not served in uniform and who had, perhaps, sensed this unwarranted insensitivity, pressed hard for a Women's Section. Eventually Earl Haig wrote to every branch Chairman urging the setting up of just this. Fortunately common sense prevailed and a number of sections for women came into being soon afterwards.

Earl Haig meeting the Central Committee of the Women's Section
at the Whitsun parade 1923.

If any doubts lingered as to the merits of women joining the Legion they were dispelled forever by the remarkable performance of these ladies selling poppies in November. They proved to be every bit as good as (and in many cases far better than) the men. Their efforts were an unqualified success and the women were here to stay, with Princess Alice as their Patron and Countess Haig as President. It soon became apparent to everyone that women were far better equipped to deal with a multitude of problems that the men either could not or would not contemplate. The creation of a maternity scheme for ex-Servicewomen was a typical case in point, with hands-on nursing and care for the wounded another.

In 1924 the Duchess of York became Patron on the retirement of Princess Alice. Far from being a mere figurehead the duchess (soon to become Queen Elizabeth, Queen Consort to King George VI) threw herself into her new role with great energy, presiding over countless meetings, touring the country and generally lifting the morale of her members at all levels. Membership increased dramatically and, come the outbreak of WWII, the Women's Section boasted more than 1,800 branches. Dispersed up and down the country these institutions were able to provide charitable and welfare work in every corner of the land. The objectives of the Section were simplified and redefined. First they vowed to support the Legion in all its activities, secondly to provide welfare for dependants of both ex-Servicemen and of the new generation of servicemen and women, and thirdly to serve the community. These objectives were achieved most successfully, not only through the darkest days of the war but in the years beyond.

After the war

The National Health Service Act of 1946 is seen by many as the beginning of the Welfare State. Would this new way of life, many asked, make the Legion redundant. To whom should ex-Servicemen now turn for help – the Legion or the State? In reply to such questions the Legion would say that it was working harder than ever before, as there were now two generations of ex-Servicemen to cater for. The Welfare State was taking time to make headway, money was, once again, tight and both fuel and food were rationed severely. Above all else, the nation was having to cope with the effects of the war on home ground which, for the first time ever, had deeply affected the civilian population throughout the United Kingdom.

In spite of all these problems the post-war era began well, commencing with the 1946 Silver Jubilee of the Legion. As well as celebrations and fund raising activities that kept the Legion in the public eye, adjustments were made to the Remembrance ceremonies, after debate about what the 11th November itself should be called and when Remembrance Sunday should be. It was decided that 11th November should be called Armistice Day, a title that remains to this day, and that Remembrance Sunday would be set always on the second Sunday in November.

The 1960 Charities Act meant that the Legion, with its near five thousand branches, had to register along with all the many other charitable organizations. This meant tax relief on monies collected but the Revenue, wanting something in return, forced changes to the wording of the Royal Charter. This, however, presented no problems:

one member of the National Council remarking wryly that the new wording rang more like Lincoln's address at Gettysburg. Where swords crossed, however, was when the Legion clashed with the Government on matters affecting service personnel. Notable victories were secured concerning forcing the Government to double the War Disability pension and to increase the financial help for war widows. Sadly, these two battles have had to be re-fought many times down the years when so often what is due to the recipients falls way behind the cost of living.

In May 1971, the Legion's Golden Jubilee, the President, General Sir Charles Jones, announced that The Queen, now Patron, had granted the prefix 'Royal' to the British Legion's title. The announcement was greeted with delight and added zest to the celebrations that year. As far as years went it was a good one but, as usual, there were problems lying in wait. WWI veterans were getting older and becoming increasingly frail, while those needing help after WWII brought added strains on the newly named Royal British Legion's finances. Membership, having soared at the end of the war, was in danger of falling away. Society was changing. Recent draconian cutbacks to the armed forces had put millions back on to the civilian job market, yet many of those released were unable to secure work. People were staying at home, more often sitting alone to watch television rather than going out for an evening's socializing. The telephone opened up new worlds, the car gave individuals freedom of movement. There was more for the young to do, but the post-war divorce rate of their parents increased markedly. Society was beginning to split and fragment. In spite of more and more people turning to the State for help, the Royal British Legion was spending every penny and more on helping those in need as the cost of care increased.

The Royal British Legion today

The Royal British Legion (RBL) today (2013) is thriving. However, like most other aged institutions, it has to move with the times. There have been problems recently and these remain, some of which are beginning to cause concern, especially at grass root level. There are now 2,500 branches and clubs up and down the country. The clubs are independent traders and, although licensed by the RBL charity, are not beholden to the welfare of the charity. However, they provide a facility for those who believe in the ethos of the RBL, and members may choose whether to join the club or not. A branch meets elsewhere, such as at a hotel, public house or TA centre. As at today, June 2013, there are slightly less than four hundred thousand members in the RBL, of whom a large number have never had any military experience.

The annual Festival of Remembrance, the Poppy Appeal and the Two Minute Silence on Armistice Day are as popular as ever, while the church service on Remembrance Sunday itself invariably fills the church to capacity – more so than on any other occasion, including Christmas Day. Added to this is the fact that the Armed Forces are regarded highly by the nation. Recent well documented operations in Iraq and Afghanistan have brought the high risk nature of military activities into the sitting rooms across the country. Casualties, while no greater, and in some cases far fewer than in previous campaigns, have been highlighted by the close attention of the media, in particular television. The nation acknowledges that it owes its young Servicemen and women a debt of gratitude and it admires them for what they do, a fact made plain by the record sales of poppies during poppy week, and by the donations made throughout the year to the RBL and other Service charities. The nation is behind the Services and their attendant charities. What, then, are the problems, and what must be done to overcome them?

Arguably the principal problem facing the RBL is its public image: it is one of gallant old gentlemen in their berets, blazers and medals marching steadily by. Such an organization is not seen by many, in particular the young, as a desirable one to join. The younger generation are indeed aware of the need to support ex-Servicemen but they do so through different organizations such as 'Help for Heroes' or 'Cash for Casualties' where they identify with those of their own age group who are being wounded in such numbers. Regimental Associations, that are doing all they can to raise money for their own, are seen by young ex-Service personnel as a more attractive alternative where they meet up once more with comrades with whom they once served. The 'Army Benevolent Fund' (The Soldiers' Charity) is run by retired officers, more as a social get together where considerable sums are raised, and is seen by many of the retired Officer corps as a more appealing alternative. It should be noted, however, that all monies raised go towards helping soldiers in distress, not officers.

As a result, many RBL branches are run by elderly members now in their late sixties or seventies. With the best will in the world, and having served their branch valiantly for years on end, many now have less energy than hitherto. They are finding it increasingly difficult to identify with the young – surely the future of the RBL. Neither do young people identify with them. Raising money with which to run the branch is often too problematical. Branch funds then dry up so the organization becomes moribund, with no scope to do anything other than meeting and drinking. In many cases the branch becomes colourless: it is not regarded as an attractive proposition and potential members go elsewhere. The vision, drive and leadership once possessed by these fine ex-WOs and S/NCOs (many branches have been run magnificently by such individuals) have dried up. Slowly but surely the branch begins to wither on the vine. Unless something is done the branch will surely die – as indeed around one a week up and down the country has closed these last four years. The RBL is losing almost seventeen thousand members a year (around fifty members a day).

Many branches, in particular the clubs that own properties, have thrown their doors wide open, in order to bring in the numbers. Membership increases (temporarily at least) and the revenue comes in, but something irretrievable is lost. The bond that draws all ex-Service personnel together, an essential part of the 'esprit de corps', is no longer there. The Service camaraderie experienced between all ranks and persuasions in bygone years has gone. In the worst cases the club premises becomes little more than a place where those who have no affiliation to the Armed Forces enjoy the cheapest beer in town.

Furthermore it is often argued that the Services, now smaller than almost ever before, can no longer provide the numbers necessary to keep branches going. But this is not so; it is simply an excuse for failing to recruit. The men and women are out there for sure. With almost fifty years of retired personnel to call upon, all but the smallest village can provide the numbers – if those identified can be persuaded to join. And here, surely, lies the root cause of the problem – the lack of fresh blood. In order to survive, the RBL has to recruit and, in particular, younger members. It will not be easy but, if the organization is to survive in its present form then this task must be addressed, and with a degree of urgency.

In order to recruit new volunteers, branches must work to a plan. Some ideas used successfully by one small branch in North Devon are shown in the next section. It takes courage for an adult to join an organization, most of whose members will be complete strangers. If it is difficult for a mature adult then it is doubly so for the younger generation and more difficult still for those still serving. Initially a room full of the grey-haired veterans with their hearing aids is an instant turn off to a young man or woman of thirty or so. However, these younger people are the ones that must be found and encouraged to join. If every branch in the land were to attract just five new members then the RBL's decline in numbers would be arrested. Once this haemorrhage has been staunched, branches will find it easier to maintain members and, indeed, for numbers to increase. An immediate advantage to this will be that the younger members will give a better public image, added to which they will want to get up and do things. Life and energy will have been breathed back: the future assured.

Clubs and branches must strive to develop a high-profile stance within the local community. Recruiting drives, jumble sales, car boot sales plus stands at local fairs and fetes where literature about themselves is on offer will surely raise their profile. Branches will be seen by the public to be alive and well. Liaison with the local Regular and TA units, as well as the cadets, is important also. The creation of a friendly relationship with the local police, paramedics, fire brigade and security companies will reap rewards, for it is to bodies such as these that many ex-Service personnel look for their second career. Such activities require time, thought and energy, however through perseverance and by refusing to take no for an answer, success will surely come.

So much for the grass roots, but problems exist at national (strategic) level. The RBL has to fight its corner in competition with countless other charities, many of whom such as the RNLI, Macmillan and Save the Children have their own devoted supporters who remain determined to catch the public's eye. In the Charity brand index for 2010, the RBL came third behind Cancer Research and the RSPCA. In the Reputation index the RBL was second behind the RNLI. However, in the Social Media league table, the Legion came first, and had the largest audience by a factor of four. These figures show that the RBL is right up there in the premier league of our national charities but, equally obvious is the fact that there is no room for complacency.

Much of today's welfare is high-tec and comes at a cost. Our National Health Service will do what it can for those in need but there comes a time when it can do no more and the patient is on his own. Electrically powered wheel chairs, chair lifts and special bath units, if they are needed, are expensive. In 2010 the total income for the RBL was £115m and expenditure £114m. In 2011 the figures were £136m and £139m respectively. Expenditure figures are bound to increase, thus the struggle to increase income, year on year, is a major concern, a constant battle. That said, income growth over the period 2006-2011 was 60 %; a remarkable achievement. But the pressure remains.

Additionally the RBL continues to be the voice of all Service personnel whereby Haig House (the RBL national Head Office) brings matters of concern to the attention of the Government. MPs in the House of Commons are made to listen, knowing full well that if action is not taken then the national media will want to know what is afoot. One notable success in 2011 was that the Prime Minister, David Cameron, promised to enshrine the principles of the Military Covenant into law, thereby guaranteeing that no members of the Armed Forces or their families should be placed at a disadvantage relative to others on account of their service – an historic breakthrough. Another success was to gain more than £40m extra in compensation for wounded and injured service personnel.

The RBL raises more money than all other service charities combined, the total for the year 2011, as we have seen, being in excess of £136m. Astonishing though this figure is, all of it and more is spent, with almost £1.5m a week going on direct welfare support alone. And last but not least, many of the clubs and branches up and down the country provide excellent focal points for those ex-Servicemen and women who are lonely and who seek companionship, or who need someone somewhere to whom they can turn. Each year the RBL responds to more than 150,000 calls for help. More than £50m has been contributed towards creating Personal Recovery Centres and a Battle Back Centre. Two new Care Centres are planned together with two further Break Centres. Add to all this the fact that the RBL liaises closely with SSAFA, Combat Stress and Help for Heroes, as well as many other service charities, and one can see that the welfare machinery at both county and national level is well tried and well proven.

Everything, it seems, is in order yet the RBL must now look to its own wellbeing. If nothing is done about improving the image and bringing in fresh blood then dark days lie ahead. The financial battle is constant, the need for new initiatives ever present. However, if these problems are addressed vigorously then a bright and rewarding future beckons – to the benefit of all concerned.

South Molton and The Royal British Legion

South Molton town

A modern map of North Devon shows the North Devon link road (A361) running north-west from Tiverton to Barnstaple. About two thirds of the way along, and lying just to the south of Exmoor National Park, is the town of South Molton. An ancient town, it may well have had its origins with the coming of the Saxons in the seventh century. That said, it was almost certainly a community of sorts much earlier. By the time of the Doomsday Book in 1086 the name had, with strong Norman influence, been changed to Sudmoltone and is recorded as belonging to the King. Later, in 1150, a Gilbert de Turbeville created the borough, a status increased to that of Royal Borough in charters signed by both Queen Elizabeth 1 in 1590, and again later by King Charles II in 1684, after he recalled many charters for revision. Even then it was known as a thriving community, and as both a centre for local agriculture and as a staging post.

South Molton played little part in the Civil War until 1655 when it was the final destination of the men who rose in Penruddock's Revolt. The rebels had ridden from Salisbury but were cornered in the town by a troop of Roundheads from Exeter. The result was a violent skirmish that took place over several hours in and around the main square. The Roundheads won the day, routing the opposition and claiming as their prize sixty Cavaliers. Throughout the seventeenth and eighteenth centuries, and even into the early nineteenth, the town prospered due to the wool trade. The elegant Georgian mill owners' houses and the mills themselves, still standing alongside the River Mole, provide clear evidence of this bygone wealth. The XVth century church of St Mary Magdelene may well be the third to be built on the site. The original church was most likely built in Saxon times because four priests are mentioned in the Doomsday Book. This early church would then have been succeeded by a later Norman church as the town grew.

The modern day parish of South Molton, with the town and parish population numbering some 4,500 inhabitants, continues to serve both the local and wider agricultural communities. The town boasts both an excellent livestock market and a busy Pannier Market which opens twice a week, once as a Farmers' Market. Local businesses associated with the agricultural and forestry industries make full use of

South Molton Town Hall

the excellent communications. Today tourism plays a larger than ever part in the economy of the town, situated as it is in an ideal position between the rugged coastline and the marvellous sandy beaches of North Devon, and Exmoor National Park.

During both World Wars, the town played its full part, losing forty-seven in WWI and a further twenty-four in WWII, all of whose names are commemorated on the town War Memorial. This sad, proud toll includes several pairs of brothers and one father and son: a true testimony to the burden borne by this small town. These figures, sobering as they are, take no account of the wounded which would have numbered almost two hundred during the first war and a further hundred in the later conflict, when the town's population was less than 3,000. Several of the more severely wounded died soon after coming home and are buried in the town cemetery. Today a number of the young men in the South Molton Branch of the RBL, who live in and around South Molton, have seen active service in the recent campaigns of Iraq and Afghanistan. One young man from nearby West Buckland was killed in action while serving in Afghanistan. A number of men who are still serving in the Armed Forces are members of the South Molton branch of the RBL.

The Royal British Legion in South Molton

The Branch was founded in 1921 along with the thousands of others nationwide. Sadly, the records of early years have been lost but the Branch, never large, thrived up to and through WWII. Reinforced after the war it lived on steadily though unspectacularly, yet seemed unable to increase membership. What numbers there were dwindled until, by the end of the fifties when the branch felt unable to continue, it ceased to exist. Mercifully Poppy Week survived during this bleak period thanks largely to a few stalwarts whose numbers included Mr Bill Webber (who later rose to become Branch Chairman) and a number of hard working ladies.

It was a Mr Roy Thompson, a tough WWII paratrooper, who reformed the Branch in the sixties, bringing in with him a number of those who had kept Poppy Week alive. Early meetings took place in a small storeroom above the Town Council offices. A Ladies Branch was formed after the war and the two branches have lived side by side ever since. Numbers, rarely above a paper strength of forty or so, produced a small but loyal hard core who brought the Branch forward successfully up to the end of the century. With no home of their own they were forced to change location between a number of public houses – a precarious and not wholly satisfactory existence. Funds to run the Branch were always tight, however members managed to get out to RBL functions, to visit other branches and to entertain at home. The Branch survived, just, but it was tough going and around the year 2000 it became apparent that the ship was starting to creak, and creak badly.

Membership had started to decline, there was little money in the kitty and the building where the Branch met was wholly unsuitable. The stairs were steep and dark, making it difficult for the elderly and impossible for the infirm. The room offered for meetings was a damp, ill-lit billiard room where members sat around the table on which a plastic sheet had been placed in order to protect the baize! It was simply not good enough. Things had to change quickly or the Branch was going to collapse once more. Not having their own property meant that the Branch always had to go cap in hand to local landlords. Eventually new premises in the town were found. A popular local hostelry offered the Branch a large room free of charge on their ground floor. There were first class facilities for the handicapped, an excellent bar and a busy restaurant, added to which there was a large car park adjacent to the establishment. 'The Coaching Inn', set close to the town centre has become the Branch's comfortable home and today members find themselves well looked after by the manageress and her staff.

Recruiting

Once in their new home things began to look up – the most pressing task now was to set about recruiting new faces. The image of the RBL did not encourage new members and the Branch was fully aware that, nationally, as shown earlier, the Legion was losing all those members every year. Furthermore, South Molton is but a small tight-knit community with jut a few satellite villages; not exactly a catchment area with potential. The first thing they did was to organize a recruiting stand right inside the Pannier Market, targeting any ex-Service personnel, in particular the young. At the same time everybody in the Branch was tasked to identify and then ask those in the 'people business' (local publicans, shopkeepers, men of the cloth, postmen and the business community) for the names and addresses of Serving and ex-Service folk. It worked. Slowly at first membership began to increase but with disappointingly few younger members.

Through perseverance the initial recruiting trickle was turned into a steady stream. Eventually, between the years 2007 and 2012, more than one hundred new faces were recruited. Most encouragingly younger members began to come forward until the Branch could claim more than forty members on their books who are aged under fifty. The average age throughout the RBL is seventy-two thus anyone under fifty is considered young, those under thirty very young indeed. New members were asked to go back and return with a friend – the reward for so doing being a bottle of champagne. This has proved to be a popular incentive and in 2010 alone, the Chairman rewarded no less than eight members with a bottle, each one bringing in a new face. New members are still coming in and, to date, membership is no longer a problem, the attendance at monthly meetings being anything between forty and over sixty.

Paying the bills

By the end of 2011, survival had been assured and success was in sight. The Branch membership was comfortable but now adequate funds needed to be accumulated so the Branch could function in a meaningful manner. Added to this, the committee had to provide entertainment for members; it was no good going to all the trouble of attracting new faces and then having nothing for them to do. In no time at all members would be voting with their feet. Branch funds were needed for two reasons, the first of which was welfare. They believed that they could help the hard pressed County Welfare team by looking after their own minor problems, either of those within the branch or indeed any ex-Service personnel living locally. If the case merited financial help then, assuming they had funds, they could react instantly. This they have been able to do on a number of occasions. Their aim is to maintain a modest welfare float, some of which is invested, with which they can answer minor calls for help.

In addition to meeting the requirements of the RBL charter, a successful branch requires its own funds to serve its own activities. It should be remembered that many of the more elderly members have no income at all other than their state pensions, sometimes but not always supplemented by further modest benefits. Life for them is not easy and the Branch helps by subsidizing the Christmas lunch and assists in chartering coaches for outings. In recent years they have visited The National Memorial Arboretum, The RN Museum at Yeovilton, the Tank Museum at Bovington and the Royal Marines at Chivenor and Norton Fitzwarren. Inviting guest speakers to give talks after meetings is always popular; recent visitors have spoken on such diverse subjects as 'The Gurkhas', 'Operations in Afghanistan', 'The Police', 'US activity in North Devon prior to D-day', 'The ascent of Everest', 'Jaguar pilots in Iraq', and more. A buffet supper concludes the evening.

Raising money for such activities is entirely separate from anything to do with Poppy Week when all proceeds go to the RBL Poppy Appeal. It is up to Branch members to raise funds for the benefit of their own Branch – by giving talks, holding raffles and bingo and by organizing events such as parties and games evenings. A major fund-raising success in 2011 was when the Branch entered and then won the prestigious RBL-sponsored 'Exmoor 3030' competition. This entailed a team of five completing a tough thirty-mile speed march over some of Exmoor's wildest and most rugged terrain. Each man had to carry thirty pounds of equipment and the total climb along the route was well over three thousand feet. The Branch team (the only RBL team to enter the competition) consisted of some of their younger serving or ex-service members. Not only did they win the event outright but they also took the prize for raising the most money (almost £10k going to the RBL and £3k to the Branch). They won again in 2012 beating fourteen other teams and setting a new record time. Any money raised by holding such events and which is considered surplus to Branch requirements goes into the Welfare fund. As a footnote to their activities in 2011, the Branch was awarded the County trophy, the Cameron-Webb cup, awarded annually to the most outstanding small branch in the county.

Keeping the show going

Maintaining attendance figures at meetings can be problematical. The Branch keeps in touch with members when they are unable to attend. Four members have served recently in Afghanistan (one in the Army Air Corps, one from 40 Cdo RM, the others with The Royal Wessex Yeomanry), and two more are soon to deploy. For these members, the pre-operational training, the leave before and after the tour, together with the tour itself takes them away for a year or more. The Branch attempts to keep in touch with these members through emails and the BFPO postal system. Other members are farmers, others in the police or security organizations and several are involved in welfare work, all of which incur a heavy time penalty.

Even with all these problems taken into account (and allowing for the occasional lapses of memory!) the Branch can guarantee a healthy turnout at every meeting, and on several occasions more than fifty percent of the paper strength have been present.

The South Molton War Memorial

Of special importance is the annual Armistice Day parade on 11th November when the Branch leads the Mayor and Town Council, together with the civilian community, in a short service at the War Memorial. The last few years have seen a turnout on parade of more than fifty members dressed for the occasion in berets, blazers and medals, and drawn up by the Parade Marshal behind their President and Branch Standard. Their own padre leads the service during which the names of those who have fallen in war are read out. The Branch plays a prominent part in the town's Remembrance Sunday church service also, when members march to church behind the Town Band and when the names of the Fallen are again read out.

Looking ahead

The South Molton Branch does not consider itself to be unusually lucky in what has been achieved. There is no luck in it, they maintain. Some years ago, when the signs were ominous, they had to brace themselves, identify what needed to be done and get on with it. They realized that nobody was going to help them – they were going to have to look after themselves. It has taken almost eight years; it has been hard work, they claim, but it has been both enjoyable and rewarding. They believe that they are now able to offer any ex-Serviceman or woman a warm and friendly welcome, and they are satisfied that they play their part as the RBL charter requires them to do. The Branch is now an established part of the community.

But they are neither complacent nor do they sit on their laurels (whatever they may be). They appreciate that, inevitably, some people move on, others move away, and eventually the oldest among them will, as the Submarine Service would say, 'slip quietly out on patrol and remain on station'. Funds have to be kept topped up – a constant challenge – and events organized. Success is sweet but has to be worked at constantly by everyone in the Branch, of whom in 2013, the eldest will be exactly one hundred years old, and the youngest but twenty-three. All, however, enjoy each others company and all regard themselves as comrades-in-arms.

That, however, is quite enough about the Branch – it is now time for you, the reader, to meet the Members themselves and to hear their stories.

The Members of the Branch

****

Taken from the poem 'A Consecration' by John Masefield (1902)

Not the be-medalled Commander, beloved of the throne,
Riding cock-horse to parade when the bugles are blown,
But the lads who carried the kopie and cannot be known.

The sailor, the stoker of steamers, the man with the clout,
The chantyman beat at the halliards putting a tune to the shout,
The drowsy man at the wheel and the tired look-out.

Theirs be the music, the colour, the glory, the gold
Mine be a handful of ashes, a mouthful of mould.
Of the maimed, of the halt and the blind in the rain and the cold –

Of these shall my song be fashioned, my tale be told. Amen.

****

Members of the South Molton Branch have each written a few hundred words on their own experiences. These are shown on the following pages, and are written entirely in their own words. The tales, of peace and war, of humour and drama, of boredom and horror, stretch from Dunkirk to Afghanistan, from the Arctic to the Equator. They are set out in alphabetical order, quite irrespective of rank, age or service. Members hail from every corner of the land, from the great towns and cities of our island, from tiny villages and the remote countryside. They neither boast nor brag, neither do they make claims of valour or victory. Rather they see themselves as the great poet would see them, as *'the lads who carried the kopie…the sailor, the stoker of steamers…the man with the clout.'*

Taken together, this is a proud record of men and women who have served their country to the best of their ability, and who are now drawn together under the banner of the RBL. It is a record of which you, the reader, can be justly proud also. You, like the poet above, may allow them to fashion your song.

****

"The safety and honour of Britain depend not on her wealth and administration, but on the character of her people". 'The Fate of the Regiment'.

Sir Arthur Bryant. April 1948.

22

George Anderson
Army. Royal Artillery. Gunner.

I was born in Elgin, North Scotland in 1945, into a military family, my father being a Sergeant in the Seaforth Highlanders who were based at Fort George, Inverness. After a full career he moved from Lichfield, Staffordshire to Birmingham where I went to school. I lived for my sport and put all my energies into them rather than my school work. I left school at fifteen. My abiding memory of those days was of my brother and I visiting our family farm back at Glenlivet in the Highlands.

I joined the Junior Leaders Regiment, Royal Artillery in 1961. It was hard work but I loved it – the discipline, the sport and a better education. I joined the Regimental band, playing the cymbals would you believe, but no matter, I was a member and had a great time touring the country doing Royal Shows and Military Tattoos. One embarrassing memory was when we were on parade in the Birmingham City Centre for the premiere of 'The Guns of Navarone'. Suddenly there was this little figure coming down the line and a Scottish voice calling out 'George…George…' It was my Mom bringing me a bag of sweeties, for Heaven's sake! I could have curled up but the sweets were good, bless her.

Then it was on to 5 Regiment R.A for adult training. One morning our Sergeant, a right hard man, was cursing and snarling that he had learned that someone had started dating his daughter, and he trusted that it was not one of us. A lot of nudge-nudge, wink-wink and foot shuffling, but little did I realize that the soldier in question was…me. I had started to see this gorgeous young girl at the local roller rink, and that evening I asked her for her second name. When she gave the answer, I almost died for it confirmed my worst fears. Nothing for it but to own up to her dad. Funnily enough we got along famously after that…I even got invited round for meals. Not such an ogre after all! But it didn't last and I was away to the King's Troop Royal Horse Artillery at St John's Wood, London. I used to see them at shows with the Junior Band

and rather fancied myself on top of a horse dashing about the place doing the musical drive. But one show season with the Troop was enough; just too much spit and polish.

By now my elder brother had joined up, he was with H Troop, 94 Locating Battery in Celle, Germany. So I transferred to join him, finding Celle a pleasant town. I landed a good job in the shape of the Troop Commander's driver/operator. I hadn't yet even passed my test so I used to drive my boss around with 'L' plates up until, one day, I drove the QM over to the Sgts Mess and immediately got my pass. Easy in those days. Yet another move saw me posted back to Bulford Camp on Salisbury Plain. Then, in 1965, came an operational tour in Borneo. Ironically, in typical Army fashion, my brother was declared medically unfit for active service due to flat feet yet, a short while later, he became a Physical Training Instructor back in Germany. Most of my time in Borneo was spent with more 'Muck than bullets'. Occasionally there was a drama but we did a number of 'hearts and minds' patrols around the surrounding villages. I celebrated my 21st there – went off on R and R with a few mates to a small island in the China Sea. We left Borneo in 1966 after the cease fire, and when in transit in Singapore, I met up with some old school chums who were with The Warwickshires en route to Borneo. What a party! I was broke but they were flush and looked after me royally in the NAAFI. Home it was by courtesy of British Caledonian where we drank the plane dry. Last but not least in my illustrious military career came with the Torrey Canyon disaster when we were sent to clean the beaches in Cornwall.

I was married by now, and shortly after was given the time honoured ultimatum – marriage or the Army. Marriage won, but only just. I decided to leave in late 1967, but realized my mistake and tried to re-enlist. However, I failed the medical with a problem that has meant several operations over the years. After leaving I did a variety of jobs – pipe fitting, milkman, erecting cranes and motorway construction. But where I really found my niche was working as a carpet estimator with a large carpet retailer. I loved it and worked for them for thirty years. My wife and I had two wonderful sons and three lovely grand daughters but unfortunately, in 1994, we divorced. I met my new partner shortly afterwards, when she was also on her own. We retired to South Molton in 2007, this being one of the better decisions of our lives, and soon afterwards I joined the South Molton Branch of the RBL. Here a great spirit of camaraderie prevails at the meetings and I feel a great sense of pride. And, like all old servicemen, I get a real 'buzz' and the chest swells proudly as we step off on parade behind the town band.

Barney Andrews
Royal Air Force Regiment. Senior Aircraftman.

My Dad had been in the RAF since well before I was born. I began life living on airforce bases in the UK and Germany. Born at RAF Strike Command, in 1979 I soon learned that Service families moved around a lot. I never really liked school: sitting in front of a board just didn't suit me. I finished with average GCSEs and vowed never, ever again, to return to a learning environment like that! Truro College in Cornwall offered me the chance of getting on the first 'public services' course to be run nationally. Designed purely around people like me, it suited me well and two years later I left with a much better qualification – plus a desire to join the forces.

Don't ask me why or how, but I bluffed my way into Nottingham University. But after failing massively for eight months, I took myself off to the Recruiting Office in the city centre. I spoke with the Royal Marines (who I'd had a crack at when eighteen, but girlfriend issues stopped play – a regret I hold even today), the Parachute Regt and the Royal Air Force. I decided whoever got back to me first would be my chosen path. In November 2000, I went to the Exeter recruiting office and spoke with an RAF Corporal – 'I'd like to be a fighter pilot', was how it started. How it ended was me agreeing to go to RAF Honington in Norfolk and attend a three day 'PGAC' course. Who and what was the RAF Regiment, I asked.

The Potential Gunners Acquaintance Course was run by Regiment Corporals. I remember the Marine Corporals were very similar. For three days we were thrashed, and out of the seventy lads starting, less than half were to begin the training. January 2001 saw me once again jumping on the train with a suitcase and heading for the start of the twenty-five week basic training to become an RAF Regt Gunner. Not a well known unit but well regarded, the RAF Regt has the second longest basic training in the UK forces. If you think it's easy, find a book about who they are and what they can do! Our training team swiftly weeded out those that weren't suitable. Week long exercises, sleep deprivation, hideously hard beastings and weapon training lasted months. Bayonet fighting, and everything else that all good soldiers learn about were covered also. Along with twelve others from the original fifty plus, I passed out as a gunner. I'd done well and was offered the choice of posting. I chose to go to 63 Squadron – The Queen's Colour Squadron.

Based at RAF Uxbridge on the outskirts of London, the process started all over again. We bulled our boots – not like before, this was a whole different level of shine. A four week drill course with an old fashioned Drill Instructor who, in hat and boots, stood well over seven and a half feet. We learned continuity drill, funeral drill and everything that went with it. We were the ones who did the silent stuff on the TV, stood outside Buckingham Palace, Windsor Castle and The Tower of London in pristine uniforms. I even got to appear on Blue Peter!

In February 2003, we were attached to 51 Squadron, RAF Regt and were deployed to Iraq for the initial ground war. We went right up the middle with the USMC and took the first objectives of the liberation of Iraq – Safwan-Jebel Senam and the Safwan airstrip. We used Landrover Wolves stripped down with no doors, roofs or windscreens. As a four man fire team the Wolf became our home - I slept in it, on it and, occasionally, under it. The drive into Iraq was under cover of darkness. The Americans and British were firing MLRS and M270 rockets, Tomahawk missiles, Abrams tanks and howitzers into the night and we were driving right through the middle of it. It smelt incredible, but what I could see is impossible to describe – millions of pounds of explosives going overhead. In the dark it was the most incredible sight I have, and probably ever will see. We carried an anti-tank weapon, a 51 mm mortar with stacks of ammunition, all types of hand grenades together with boxes and boxes of ammo, plus our water and food.

Driving through a minefield, we set off an anti-tank mine which only partially detonated. Had it gone off properly we, by all accounts, would have been vapourised. Instead it removed our front nearside wheel, depositing it a few hundred metres away. Had we been heavier my story would have been written by my father - I'd not be here. We raided houses looking for Ba'ath party members, hid in sniper positions observing the enemy from within the village, and often donned full NBC gear after endless gas warnings.

Back home again after six months, I'd done what I wanted to do in the forces, deciding that my nine lives had been used up very quickly. I left and joined the police where I remain today. I am a motorcyclist, a traffic cop and an ex-firearms officer. I'm married and have a baby daughter. I loved my time in the Regiment and now, through the RBL, I'm able to talk to other lads who have become good friends, about things that only we can understand.

The Reverend Bob Andrews
Royal Air Force. Chaplains' Branch. Wing Commander.

Only seen now in aviation museums, wartime aircraft flew much lower and slower than their modern equivalents. Schoolboys of the time were experts at aircraft recognition, and easily distinguished the Havard trainer from the Hurricane fighter, the twin engined Anson from the Oxford, or the four engined Stirling, Halifax or Lancaster. Living in the Midland countryside, and on the edge of wartime activity, one could lie in bed listening to the menacing throb of German bombers heading for the industrial towns, and see the night sky glowing from the fires miles away.

Born in 1933, I joined the RAF in 1954, serving first as an ambulance driver at the Sunderland Flying boat station at Pembroke Dock. Then to Germany, based at Gutersloh and then to Nordhorn, where, as a heavy goods driver, I saw much of Western Germany still working hard to recover from its wartime devastation.

Acceptance for training to the Anglican priesthood was followed by four years at residential Theological college, and five years as curate to the large parish of Kingswinford in the West Midlands. In 1969 I rejoined the RAF as a chaplain and went as junior chaplain to RAF Cranwell. The senior padre at the time was an old Harrovian who had trained as a pilot with the Fleet Air Arm. Now qualified to fly RAF aircraft, he sometimes gave me the opportunity to accompany him as he flew a Jet Provost trainer. Within a few weeks of my first posting as solo padre to RAF Odiham, two helicopters collided over the airfield, killing five men with whom I had just had lunch. This was a baptism of fire into the grief of young families, military funerals and the intense administrative procedures.

From Odiham back to Germany as chaplain to RAF Larbruch, a front line Cold War station flying Phantom and Buccaneer aircraft in constant readiness for strike action as and when necessary. A curious highlight was getting to meet a fierce little Air Marshal who had made military history as Flight Lieutenant Mickey Martin, a surviving Lancaster pilot of 617 Squadron Dam Busters fame, who did not suffer fools gladly or otherwise. Posted back to RAF North Luffenham in Rutland, an Air Traffic Radar Control Centre and a 'Need to Know' Russian language school, the padre was also vicar to the local parish of Edith Weston. On the edge of what is now called Rutland Water, it was then a valley of agriculture, farms and houses.

Three and a half years as chaplain to Strike Command at High Wycombe was both interesting and demanding, lively and entertaining, mainly because of the wide variety of branches, trades and personnel represented by an equally wide rank structure. It was also quite helpful to be able to quickly identify the uniformed top brass of weekdays, but who were now the civilian-suited worshippers in my Sunday congregation! Another move to RAF Abingdon where the Jaguar strike aircraft was serviced, and also home to the Oxford and London University Air Squadron flying Chipmunk and Bulldog trainers, found me once again vicar of the local parish of Shippon. The annual Air Day was a very exciting event, but the quiet arrival of the Battle of Britain Flight Lancaster for its annual major service was even more so. My family and I were given the opportunity to climb inside; a real experience of history.

Eventually, following a short posting to the technical training school at RAF Locking near Weston Super Mare, it was back to Germany, this time to the huge NATO headquarters at Rheindhalen near Munchengladbach, which included the RAF hospital at Wegberg. The fine Army-run church was shared with the RAF and, depending upon the personalities involved at any one time, worked well. Within my first year, there occurred a catastrophic road accident on the Munich Autobahn. Twenty-two RAF bandsmen and a policeman along with the German driver of the coach they were travelling in, were killed in the fireball after the coach hit a tanker fully laden with aviation fuel. Featuring for days and weeks in newspaper headlines and TV news bulletins, the tragedy was hard to handle. Although most of the deceased were repatriated to their hometowns, a joint service for five men was held in the station church. Inevitably the work of ministry and counselling to the many young families, along with massive administration, and memorial services and concerts occupied much of the remaining time.

My final posting to RAF St Mawgan in Cornwall, hosting Nimrod Maritime squadrons and also the beginnings of what is now Newquay Airport, was fairly uneventful, but a good introduction to this rugged but beautiful county. Most of the married quarters were situated at St Eval, built on the remains of a very active wartime Coastal Command Station. The remote church is now a shrine of memory to all who flew, served and died during those years.

Leaving the RAF and appointed rector of St Just in Roseland with St Mawes, we enjoyed this 'area of outstanding natural beauty' along with the great and the good who often visited for a few days of peace and privacy. Hosting Prime Minister Thatcher, husband Dennis plus entourage for coffee, we removed the gift copy of 'Spycatcher' by Peter Wright from our bookshelves. She had tried to ban its publication, so having glanced at our bookshelves, she failed to find it! A crisis was narrowly avoided, but then our Labrador, having found the waiting coffee arrangements had polished off the cream!

As the oldest Royal British Legion chaplain in Devon, I think I will now award myself a medal….

*****

Kevin Bateman
40 Cdo Royal Marines. Colour Sergeant.

Born in 1973, I was seventeen when I had my first run in with the Royal Marines, when I went along to the Recruiting Office. The guy there wasn't interested with who I was or what, just how many pull-ups I could do. I did eight and was told to come back when I could do eighteen. Well, before I knew it, I found myself arriving by train at the CTCRM. Hadn't a clue what to expect but a few weeks earlier I had got into a fight when this bloke grabbed my hair, so I had it all shaved off. Anyway I had a baseball cap on and this bloody great marine told me to get the effing thing off – sharpish! I did. He took one look and told me to get the effing thing back on again. Welcome to the marines!

Anyway I somehow made it through the selection and, on 22 Oct 1990, arrived for training. One hell of a shock, so it was, but I hung on in, living each day as it came along. Come Week 19 and we found ourselves in a field with all our kit; everything - beds, lockers the lot. Why so, we had no idea. We didn't ask (you never did), just did what we were told. Then the screaming started, telling us to get all our stuff out of the lockers and into the kit bags. Then came the fun – a little game called 'Helicopters' that the training team plays. Over to the estuary we doubled and emptied the kit bag into the thick, stinking mud. Thrashed through the mud for an hour or so, then picked up our kit and returned to our billet. There I was, standing by my bed covered in mud, when one of the trainers came in. We snapped to attention and awaited our fate. So…now we became helicopters and whirled a piece of our kit around our heads. Seconds earlier the room had been immaculate but then the mud and the s… flew, decorating the place beautifully. Thirty minutes to clean the place up for room inspection. Hello and welcome again!

Well, I passed out of training and on to 42 Commando Royal Marines in Bickleigh, Plymouth. Great – there I was, young, fit and ready to go. Nobody spoke to me for ages, until we began to get ready for Northern Ireland. This was to rural Fermanagh where I was a member of a small patrol in Support Company. We had a number of incidents and a few guys were wounded, but no fatalities. After the tour came a jolly in the Med. A real boy's holiday, it was, and I was getting paid for it. Overdid it once. There I was in Cyprus, the wrong side of the island, in some bird's bed and I should have been back in camp. I managed to find a mad Cyp with his Merc who raced me back across the island. Got away with it so tried it again. Didn't make it this time and took a hammering from the Sergeant Major. Fair one. But he wasn't all bad 'cos, after he'd smashed me and banned my shore leave, he asked me if she was worth it all. Answer, yes, I'd pulled an absolute cracker and was living the dream. He told me to get out but I knew that he was thinking of his own younger days when he'd done just the same – or worse. Bootnecks we are, hoofing it about the place.

I was based at 42 Commando for a number of years in the early nineties. It was great – the summers seemed like holidays abroad, and when we were off it was to places like the Med. Just after the Northern Ireland tour I decided I was going to be an Assault Engineer. Basically speaking this meant blowing things up for a living and I reckoned that'd be pretty darned good – what better for a young Marine. Life was great again and, somehow, I made it to Corporal within the branch. It was then that we went to Sierra Leone when the West Side Boys were strutting their stuff. Well, we soon sorted them – no problem. I've gone on since then and loved the job in every rank. Travelled around the world a number of times – did my Winter Warfare in Norway and jungle training in Brunei and Belize. Have made some great mates along the way.

My last tour was with 40 Cdo when we were deployed to Afghanistan for Op Herrick 12 in 2010. In one respect it was a good tour in that we did a lot for the civilian community, but it was hard too. Sadly we lost twenty-one from the Battle Group, including fourteen lads from the unit; something we will never forget. My job was adviser to the CO and to make sure the lads knew of any updates in the enemy's techniques or devices. We all had a few close shaves, a few times I got a bit close to a couple of our 1,000 pounders going off. Memories remain, like the time when I found myself close to an enemy firing point and seeing the grenades coming in. Another long day, but there we are. Scary at times, but when you're there you just get on with it.

Anyway, I'm now a C/Sgt with twenty-one years under my belt. I'm on my last posting now – down at Plymouth at *HMS Drake* Naval Base. I enjoy being in the RBL. We've got a great branch and I've met some good mates from other units.

*****

Pat Brend
Women's Royal Naval Service. Writer.

I was born in east London in 1937 where my family consisted of Mum, Dad who was in the Merchant Navy, and my younger sister.

I was around four years old when the war started and I experienced going down to the shelter in the back garden every time the siren went, and listening to the flying bombs and holding my breath until they passed. I also remember standing on the front door step with my parents (Dad was on leave) watching the 'dog-fights' above us with planes swooping around the sky with the roar of their engines. I suppose it could have been part of the Battle of Britain but I was too young to realise. I must have been fascinated with the sounds and spectacle of it and even the excitement, but never thought that we could be in any sort of danger.

We were never evacuated but my Mum used to take us both down to Combe Martin regularly to stay with an elderly aunt. I am not sure if Mum was worried about Gran being so close to the Blitz because Gran flatly refused to leave London.

As to joining the Navy, I always used to say to my school friends that I was going to join up when I was old enough. At that time they also agreed to do the same. I have always had an urge to go out and do positive things and not just sit back and let things happen. I just wanted to be the master of my own destiny, I suppose. It seemed that it was something that I had to do. When I became old enough at age 17, I joined the WRNS but my friends by then had all changed their minds!

My initial training was at Reading where I enjoyed being in a military environment with the inevitable discipline, and being exposed to the challenges that went with it, and generally learning to work as a team member. But also to use my initiative and be able to stand on my own two feet. It was good grounding for my future life. On my Part 1 training we had a visit from the Queen Mother and I was part of the Guard of Honour.

After that I was posted to *HMS Ceres* for my Writers' course which I enjoyed. I ended my three years service at MOD London where I got married to John who I had met earlier at Combe Martin. He was in the RAF Police and, after our wedding, he spent some time in Aden and then Chivenor where we made our home. After a long and happy life, and after John died in 2006, I moved to Bishops Nympton where I live in retirement. I joined the South Molton RBL for companionship and have made a number of good friends.

*****

Patrick Brook
Army. Sultan of Oman's Armed Forces. Colonel.

Many years after arriving in this world back in 1940, I found myself as a troop leader in an Armoured Regiment in Germany. The prospect of spending most of my service life there was very depressing and I was determined to find an alternative. My regiment, The Royals, had previously sent an officer on secondment to the Sultan's Armed Forces, and a close friend had recently completed a happy tour there as leader of a troop of camels. Camels sounded more interesting than Centurion tanks, so I volunteered. The regiment would survive without me so I was dispatched to Beaconsfield to learn Arabic. Our small class of six included two Marines and the intrepid explorer Sir Ranulf Fiennes who I had known earlier.

Mid-1968 saw me in Muscat as 2 i/c of a rifle company of the Muscat Regiment. My romantic ideas of taking camels into the wastes of the Empty Quarter were dispelled as soon as I learned that the Sultan's Armed Forces were fighting a very serious war against communist backed tribesmen in their Dhofar Province, adjoining what is now Yemen. The Dhofari tribesmen were formidable; they knew the terrain and were skilled marksmen. Many had been sent to Russia and China for training, and were taught to use the heavy weapons that were being supplied, such as the Katyusha rocket and Shpagin machine gun.

Many others had been trained by the British Army whilst serving in the Dhofari Squadron of the Trucial Oman Scouts in the Gulf. I had served there for a short time prior to my secondment to Oman. When there, a Dhofari Sergeant in my squadron told me that he was returning to Dhofar for his leave. Several months later he surrendered to me, walking in with six anti tank mines and the leave pass which I had signed. He apologised for being late!

In early 1969 we were deployed for an operational tour of Dhofar and my company was given the task of establishing a position close to the Yemeni border. The position was called Defa and was without doubt the most unattractive, inhospitable and dangerous place imaginable. We were constantly shot up by the enemy (the addoo) with small arms fire and mortars. Our greatest problem was the lack of water as there were no water holes apart from those in enemy territory. The nearest supply was a hundred miles away to where we ran a weekly water convoy. This entailed a drive across the desert along tracks which were mined – on average we lost one vehicle on every resupply. However when we had enough water we had to get on with our task. This meant patrolling into the tree line which provided excellent cover but was extremely difficult to move in, with visibility down to a few yards.

On our position at Defa we had one Vickers machine gun and a 25 pounder artillery piece to provide supporting fire. The addoo usually shot us up at us at last light. The Vickers was a belt fed machine gun which saw service in the First World War. It had a range of 2,000 yards which greatly exceeded anything used by the enemy. We decided to take our Vickers out on patrol and I was tasked with looking after the weapon and its tripod which was strapped on to two donkeys, each with a handler.

Our aim was to move through the undergrowth to the edge of the escarpment which led down to the sea. On one occasion after supper, we saw what we thought were vehicle headlights on the horizon. It later transpired that the enemy was using an old Land Rover to carry supplies along a camel track. However nothing; the operation was uneventful and was called off. When we were within a kilometre of camp we came under heavy small arms fire from the addoo, who were behind us. We took cover, and in the ensuing chaos I failed to see that our donkeys, plus our trusty Vickers, had vanished. Eventually the firing stopped and I looked around for the donkey handlers. However, they were looking for the donkeys who had vanished in the direction of the enemy. The handlers reported gleefully that the donkeys had disappeared into the trees and that the addoo would, by now, be preparing our Vickers for action.

Disconsolately, we trudged back to Defa, a more depressing situation difficult to imagine. The handlers were still with me and I told them to go back to the donkey lines. A few seconds later there was a shout of 'Al Hamdulillah' (thanks be to God). The donkeys were safe and sound, as were their loads. What a relief! How quickly can one move from hell to heaven!

Five years later I returned to Defa under very different circumstances. I was in command of the Armoured Car Squadron and liaison officer with the Iranian Army. The Iranians provided a brigade of infantry with supporting arms to assist in establishing blocking positions between Defa and the sea. But the war, by now, was drawing to a close. The Iranians were poorly trained with many conscripts yet they provided the essential boots on the ground. Their losses were never revealed but were, for certain, very heavy. On one contact alone the addoo overran an Iranian position and killed every one, but ten yards from the sangar I was crouching in. We loaded the ten bodies into the casevac helicopter. I have always felt that insufficient credit has been give to the Iranians for their substantial contribution to the successful conclusion of this little known war.

Mike Buckland
Royal Air Force. Pilot. Flight Lieutenant.

I was born in Chippenham on 11th July 1969. My father was a farmer, my mother's family originated from Baku in Azerbaijan. I started school in Newton Abbot and then went on to King's Bruton and Kelly where I lived for my sport, in particular rugby, tennis and cross country. I was awarded an RAF Flying Scholarship and joined the RAF in 1987, graduating from Cranwell the following year. First stop was RAF Church Fenton learning about jets with the Jet Provost, first going solo aged eighteen. Then came the Advanced Fast Jet Training at RAF Valley in North Wales where I flew the Hawk T1. I completed the course and was awarded my wings when just twenty.

My first tour was at RAF Wyton in Cambridgeshire, flying the Canberra with 100 Squadron. I flew several varieties of the aircraft in the recce, target and intercept roles. Six months a year was spent in Cyprus at RAF Akrotiri in the target towing and intercept role for the Phantom and Tornado F3 air defence squadrons. Pretty tedious but somebody had to do it! Back to 100 Squadron and we were re-rolled with the Hawk and moved to RAF Finningley carrying out intercept sorties at both high and low level. Then it was back to Valley again to complete my Tactical Weapons Training. From there I was sent to RAF Cottesmore where I flew the Tornado GR1 in the ground attack role. After a short tour with 15 Squadron up at RAF Lossiemouth, Scotland I was off to RAF Germany to RAF Bruggen in the Strike/Attack role. Whilst here I was Combat Ready in both the Ground Attack and Nuclear Strike role. We specialised in Thermal Imaging and Laser Designation, which involved dropping the Paveway Laser Guided Bombs. Then came Iraq.

We flew from Bruggen to Incirlik in Turkey from where we covered both northern and mid Iraq, and from Saudi Arabia and Kuwait where we reached out to cover both south and mid Iraq. These missions consisted of both reconnaissance and targeting of Iraqi Surface to Air Missile systems (SAMs) and the movement and deployment of ground based equipment. The missions would involve up to forty coalition aircraft in a variety of roles and were flown every day and night of our operational tour. On a number of sorties we were targeted by SAMs and other AAA sights. On one occasion my navigator asked about 'those funny black clouds up ahead'. The answer was that we were flying into flak. On almost every mission my radar warning receiver told me that we were under SAM attack. On another occasion, we had to make an emergency 'Mayday' landing in Kuwait when one of the engines on our Tornado GR1 had packed up. A bit dicey but it was what we had trained for and we revelled in it.

Doing all this and living in fifteen man tents in fifty degrees C, together with the dreaded desert sand and all its creepy crawlies, a very strong sense of humour was necessary. So…one day, in order to improve our living conditions, they gave us a wooden floor (in pieces, mind you) along with the nails and tools for the job. Get on with it, they said. HM's finest aircrews then set about the carpentry but failed completely, leaving themselves with no wood left over yet a very large hole in the middle of the floor. Funnily enough everybody else got it right. Anyway, with little else to do while waiting for the next mission, we fished through the hole with biscuits on pieces of string for the desert mice.

Back in Germany at the end of it all we were involved in endless NATO exercises with other nations. Large formations of international aircraft and squadrons flew together and against each other in enormous war games. Sometimes it was pretty close to the wire and we would land wide eyed and with a few more grey hairs. After this I was posted back to 208 Squadron at RAF Valley as an Instructor. I and a dozen others were responsible for thirty students. While here they were taught to fly the Hawk, a new experience as the basic trainer was now the Tucano. This aircraft, whilst modern, was propeller driven, a very different beast from the much faster jet. The speed of the Hawk compared to the Tucano was the main obstacle for the students, something they had to overcome quickly in order to advance on the course. On more than one occasion we found ourselves wrestling the controls away from the student as he or she did their best to pile drive us both into the ground. After Valley came Coltishall to No 6 Squadron with the Jaguar GR3A. The Jaguar was the first RAF fast jet to be equipped with the helmet mounted sight, allowing the pilot to target ground and air threats through sightline.

Come July 2003 and I came down to earth with a bump, struck by a virus that attacked my heart and left me with severe cardiac cardiomyopathy. Eventually, when partially recovered, I was sent to Boscombe Down where I ran the Eurofighter (Typhoon) desk which required me to produce the handling and emergency procedures for the RAF's latest multi role aircraft.

I was invalided out of the RAF in 2003 and now live in South Molton with wife, Debbie, and two beloved cockers – Jade and Conker. My cockpit now is a desk in 'Seddons', an estate agency in Dulverton, while Debbie is a Community Nurse. I joined the RBL in 2009 with precious little knowledge of what they did even! I have since been quite overwhelmed by the friendship and camaraderie shown by both young and old, and the often noisy, cheerful and eventful meetings.

*****

Adrian Budd
Royal Navy. Engineer. Chief Petty Officer.

Born in 1963, I was always keen to join the Navy. My father was in the Royal Navy, serving on Motor Torpedo Boats, *HMS Chieftan* and *HMS Boxer*, and would often tell us stories of life in the navy. My entire family, for generations, have been at sea in one way or another, mainly on trawlers, as most of them are from Grimsby. When I was just fourteen I sailed with the trawlers Rose Kashmir and Rose Kelly to Spitsbergen, Tromso and the White Sea. On 2nd May 1980, I joined *HMS Fishguard*, in Torpoint.

It all came as a shock and I found the first year really tough - even the kitbag seemed to weigh a ton! The final three years of my apprenticeship were in Scotland, across the Forth from Edinburgh at *HMS Caledonia*. During this period the Falklands war broke out and I joined shifts in the dockyard loading craft with stores for those down South. Ironically I was storing a trawler from Hull where most of the stores was beer! I did some training on some real old ships – *HMS Duncan, Eastbourne* and *Kent* and finally got to sea on *HMS Fearless*. There were some interesting visits for us including a memorable one to Split and Istanbul.

I finally joined my first ship *HMS Brilliant* as a Leading Hand in 1984 and set off to see the world. My next ship was *HMS Boxer* which I joined in 1986, great to join a ship with the same name as one my father had served on. It was a happy time for me and I learned much about engineering, especially the Rolls Royce Gas Turbine that formed our main propulsion system. Then came the Iran/Iraq war and we spent many weeks patrolling off the Gulf States. During one episode we were on the upper deck at lunchtime when a couple of lads wearing full anti-flash and overalls ran past us and hastily loaded a chaff launcher with anti-missile decoys. We asked them what the hurry was. Nothing much…just that an incoming missile had been picked up heading for us. Having got below sharpish, we heard that the missile had struck an Esso tanker. Memories mainly of having to wear special white overalls to bed – in case we were attacked by missiles. Not pleasant, especially in the heat of the Straits of Hormuz. Then came the Bosnian crisis when we were tasked to stop and board countless ships.

I next spent a few years engineering on shore in Plymouth dockyard. My next ship – *HMS Cornwall* – was absolutely beautiful – a stunning ship that was launched by HRH The Princess of Wales. I remember chatting to her when she came round to meet the crew. Come the second Gulf War and we found ourselves escorting British registered tankers and giving assistance to those that had been damaged. But despite traveling the world, the highlight would be our many trips to London where the Guild of Leathersellers looked after us wonderfully well. After *HMS Cornwall* I returned to Plymouth Dockyard and then joined *HMS Beaver*. It was in 1998, a lovely hot summer and I'd just met Amanda who would later become my wife. *HMS Beaver* was a bit of an old girl by that time and, on the day I left, she was committed for scrap! And yet, despite all her troubles we were never late sailing and always got in on time, if not earlier!

In 1997 we had a memorable deployment where Ho Chi Min City and Hong Kong were the highlights. I also managed to get a couple of weeks off when my girl friend came over to see me. We had a fantastic holiday and got engaged, then married on my return. Eventually I became bored at sea so decided to study, including horticulture. When in port, I would often be found in parks and gardens whilst the rest of the crew were in pubs. On one occasion in Gib, I bumped into the captain. He looked astonished and when, a few months later, I gained a distinction it was broadcast over the loud speaker to the whole ship's company! I also studied Business studies, commerce and biology, managing good grades. All this got me thinking – perhaps there was more to life than the navy. For the Business studies, I drew up a business plan. It seemed to work so I turned it into a real one. On leaving *HMS Beaver*, my wife and I bought four run down flats in one house near the dockyard and started a company called Haddington House apartments. I was then ashore working as a coppersmith.

The holiday business, work and family kept us really busy and after three years ashore I was shocked to receive the draft back to sea. I'd been told to start looking for another job when I got to forty and, with just a couple of years left, had hoped to stretch my shore time to the end. Not so, and with about six months to go before my fortieth birthday and release, the captain sent for me. He said the navy wanted to keep its most experienced engineers and that I had been accepted as one of them. No way, and it was gratifying to be able to turn down this career extension. My colleagues, however, thought I was mad!

In 2006 we bought our farm in North Devon. Our latest venture 'The Cast Iron Air Brick Company' which we started in 2009 is going from strength to strength and now sells cast iron vent grilles to property restorers worldwide. Recent customers have included Baroness Thatcher, Buckingham Palace and even the London Olympics. We also have a couple of holiday cottages. Life remains busy!

*****

Ernie Chanter
Army. Royal Army Medical Corps. Private.

I was born in South Molton on 1st March 1919. Very soon after this great event, my father came into town to collect mother and I in a horse drawn buggy and took us home to the village of Bishops Nympton. I spent all my early life there, leaving the village school at fourteen. During my last two years at school, I was expected to help make the bread for the family bakery. Later, in 1939, the family moved to South Molton to set up their business. It was September, the same month that war broke out.

Almost immediately I received my call up papers. Volunteering to be a baker, I was ordered to report to No 11 Casualty Clearing Station as a medic. Quite amazing! I hadn't the faintest idea about what to do. But I soon found out. In March the following year we were deployed to France as members of the B.E.F. All was quiet until 10th May when the German 'Blitzkrieg' began and we moved up to Belgium. Quite early on we began to receive casualties but were forced back to La Panne just north of Dunkirk. We still tried to work in our three operating teams but it became increasingly difficult. Life got steadily worse. Many of the casualties were in a truly horrific condition, the worst, as I remember, being as a result of shell splinters. Wounded patients were brought in and operated where they were, on their stretchers on the floor, with the blankets often blood soaked and reeking. We buried the dead where we were. It was a nightmare. Eventually we were ordered to destroy our equipment and it was a case of 'Every man for himself – do your best and good luck'.

It was not at all pleasant on the beaches either, my worst memory being of the Stukas dive bombing with their sirens screaming: that and the continual shell fire. Some men went mad with terror. We were often in the water for hours on end. Eventually a destroyer came in and we managed to get on board by using the scrambling nets, with nothing but the clothes we stood up in. I distinctly remember the sailor who hauled me aboard saying 'Come on, soldier – we're taking you home'. On the ground and in the water it was chaos but on board it was mercifully calm – thank God for the Navy! On arrival in England we re-assembled and were despatched to Porthmadog to lick our wounds. And it was near here that I met my lovely wife – Jane. It was one evening during a total blackout that I was fumbling for the telephone when this voice said 'Hello'. Later, and still in complete darkness, she bade me farewell. Without pausing to think I asked her to the pictures the following night. She obliged and three weeks later we were engaged.

After an uneventful spell we were issued with tropical kit and rumour had it that we were going to Iceland. Not so – after embarking at Liverpool our convoy of some thirty ships sailed for the Middle East, most of us surviving a number of U-boat attacks in the Atlantic. Eventually we disembarked at Port Taufiq and moved up to join the Eighth Army. My most abiding memory of life in the desert was of the terrible flies that were forever swarming over you, your food and your water. Eventually we moved back to Haifa where we embarked for the invasion of Italy.

We landed at Bari and immediately set up our Casualty Clearing Station (CCS) behind the front line. Military operations were continuous as we made our way up through Italy. Work in the CCS never seemed to slacken and, although never callous or indifferent to the terrible sights and sounds of the wounded, we became hardened to it, none the less – we had to. There was one occasion when I was in the Operating Theatre and the surgeon said quite casually 'OK. Finished, sew him up'. To which the anaesthetist replied equally casually 'Too late, chum – he's gone'. No time to stop and think about it – the next patient was being carried in.

VE Day for me was in Milan where everybody celebrated in spectacular fashion – the Italians were particularly friendly. Our driver, long since quite incapable of driving anything, eventually collapsed on to the ground muttering 'Can't drink any more… just pour it over me!' Disgraceful really, but it had been a very long time indeed and the relief of it being all over was really something. Eventually we reached Austria. It was now 1945 and after three and a half years away from home I applied for leave – sending a telegram to Jane 'Have leave…prepare for wedding'. We were married on 22nd August after which I returned until the end.

Demob for me came a year later, when I came back home and joined my father in the family bakery business where I remained until retirement. I now live with my daughter – Dawn – in South Molton and enjoy getting along to the RBL Branch meetings when I can. Looking back on it all, one's memories are very mixed. Some memories are truly horrible, flashbacks I would happily forget if I could. But other recollections are really happy, in particular of the wonderful friendships that were struck up in those far off days and which still endure today. I suppose that I went through quite a bit, but looking back I seem to have had a charmed life – lucky, very lucky.

*****

Tony Chapman
Royal Navy. Leading Telegraphist.

As a young boy of sixteen, an Air Raid Precaution (ARP) volunteer, I looked out over the docklands of Southampton, my home town, as the Luftwaffe carried out their destructive bombing raids on the city during 1940 to 1941. It was certainly an experience and I expect that there were many youngsters of a similar age to myself, who felt the same raw excitement of war.

 Perhaps I was 'case hardened' prior to volunteering for service with the Royal Navy at age seventeen. I had intended, perhaps with the naivety of youth, to be a Submariner, away from enemy bombers, but the Navy had other ideas and I was trained as a Radio Operator with the elite Coastal Forces and subsequently as a Visual Signaller, otherwise known in the trade as a 'Bunting Tosser'.

My first draft was on a Motor Torpedo Boat (MTB) and Motor Launches (ML) which were actually gunboats, tiny by comparison with other ships of the Fleet but heavily armed for their size and packed a real punch. The conditions on board were cramped to say the least and 13 of us lived, ate and slept in a very small area filled with all the aroma of bodies, fuel and the galley close by. However it moulded us into a close and efficient fighting team.

Having ploughed a consistent furrow around Portland Bill and the Isle of Wight, I experienced Radar Detection Finding (RDF) for the first time, when I received a signal telling us exactly what our position was. The system was not installed in our ship, sheer magic! We subsequently joined patrols in the North Sea and it was here that we became involved in an attempted attack on one of our northern bound convoys by some thirty German E Boats, out of Dutch and Belgian ports. Together with *MGB 603* we made contact with six E Boats and sank three, during which *MGB 607* was disabled having half the crew killed or wounded. Our boat had actually cut through one German vessel, described by our skipper as 'like a knife through butter'. I had been rendered unconscious at that particular time and I was told of it later! The incident was subsequently published in the London Illustrated News.

In 1944 I was drafted to *HMS Nile*, HQ Eastern Mediterranean, and remained at this location until hostilities ceased. We were involved in some interesting jobs such as landing agents, Greek commandos, a nasty bunch but great allies, or just looking for something to sink. When the moon was high we patrolled the coast near Beirut, Haifa and up to Palestine which was particularly hostile to our activities. On one patrol we were diverted to search for a Greek minesweeper whose crew had mutinied and imprisoned the officers. We located the ship and 'invited' them to surrender or we would immediately dispatch them to their 'Maker'. They opted for surrender but it was really 'Hobson's Choice' as they would, in all probability, face a firing squad when we landed them at Alexandria. Another trip was to pick up four German spies and take them to the same destination. They were all roped together and there was no shortage of volunteers to guard the prisoners as one was a 'humdinger' of a young woman and it was a long time since we had seen a female!

Towards the end of the war we could roam the seas at will, in daylight. We used the narrow Kos straight staying close to the Turkish side for safety and on one occasion the German garrison signalled, in perfect English suggesting that we come a little closer. I replied by Aldis Lamp 'no thanks' and suggested that he should come out to us. Their request was repeated and I signalled in reply, what was an appalling lie 'we have enjoyed a lovely breakfast of sausages and 'train smash' what did the Fuhrer send you?' End of exchange!

On one occasion we were tasked to land humanitarian aide to the islanders of Khalkia on the Rhodes coast. We had done similar work but this time it was a day light operation, close to a German garrison and not a particularly good idea. We could not enter the tiny harbour so our 'Number One' was put ashore in a dinghy to unload provisions when quite unexpectedly, literally out of a clear blue sky, a shell landed. As we could not enter the small harbour we sat tight and watched the gun flashes. It was 'several weeks' before the 'Number One' returned having plotted the precise position of the gun battery and, incredibly, we had not been hit! But the Germans had made a big mistake as a month later we returned at night with a party of Greek Commandos. There was no battery in operation after that!

Looking back I can honestly say that I enjoyed my time in the Royal Navy, even the excitement and danger of active service. I held no grudge against the enemy whom I came into close contact with on several occasions, neither did I feel any particular emotions when I watched a young German sailor being hauled out of the sea to breathe his last breath on deck in front of me. He had done his duty and I was doing mine, nothing more nothing less. Perhaps the young ARP volunteer who had watched the destruction of his home town had become immune to the horror of war.

My final association with the Services continued during the Cold War, when I joined the Royal Naval Auxiliary Service, becoming Head of the North Devon Unit and Skipper of Auxiliary Craft. Our role was to train for the job of shepherding merchantmen to special anchorages and to form up convoys on the assumption that our main ports would have been nuclear targets. It was extremely interesting and a pleasant diversion from a busy professional life, but that, as they say, is a different matter.

*****

Phylis Cheek
Army. Auxiliary Territorial Service. Corporal.

I was born in 1913 in a house we shared with my Aunt and Uncle's family in Paddington. My earliest memory is of a Zeppelin raid on the aircraft factory producing Sopwith Camels, where my mother worked. When my father returned from the First World War, he secured a job as a night watchman and we moved to Peabody Buildings in Mayfair. I left school in 1927, the year after the Great Strike during which I remember armoured cars being deployed, and started work for a photographer in Bond Street. During the Great Depression, I was unemployed for a while but then worked in Woolworths before getting a job as a dancer at the Prince of Wales Theatre.

In Jan 1942 I received my call up papers and volunteered for the A.T.S. – I didn't want the WAAFs as they were only after cooks. It was a relief to get away from the blitz and to be sent for basic training somewhere peaceful. I was stationed in Droitwich and was there for three months. We were billeted in a hotel but were forbidden to use the bar! I was then transferred to Kingston to start tuition as a telephonist, my only memory of that was being on duty most of the night stoking the boilers. Once trained I was posted to Seaford in the Gun Ops room. I used to take messages from Fighter Command in Uxbridge and do the plotting of enemy aircraft in the Channel Sector. After the victory at Alamein I was transferred to a holding unit awaiting transportation to the Middle East: this was in Bayswater, so at least I could get home.

In Feb 1943 we were taken by blacked-out train to a secret destination. It was Olympia which I recognized immediately I opened the window. We journeyed on to Liverpool and embarked on the 'Cape Town Castle' sailing for Greenock where we waited at sea for the convoy to assemble. We then sailed all the way round Africa to Egypt via Freetown and Durban. On 1st March U-boats were sighted in the North Atlantic and we went to emergency stations. For three days we never got out of uniform, and there were four of us girls in a tiny cabin. However we were never allowed on deck as the men were sleeping there. All in all we were twenty girls to over a thousand men but we were classed as Warrant Officers thus had better accommodation than most.

We disembarked at Port Taufiq in Egypt on 15th April 1943 and entrained to Cairo, where we were billeted in Kasernill Barracks. Here I operated the switchboard before being hospitalized with Sand Fly Fever. Then it was off to Alexandria which was beautiful, doing the same duties and where I met Donnie. We had a whirlwind romance and lots of fun. Once some boys from the RAF gave me a lift in a bomber, sitting on the floor, as I wanted to get up to Cairo for some leave to see him. When Italy capitulated, my friends and I celebrated a bit too much. We were caught climbing the barrack gates in the early hours, for which I got seven days and was demoted from Corporal back to Private. In Nov 1944 I was discharged so I could return to the UK and have my son. Donnie was already there, convalescing before being posted to Germany.

We continued living in London after the war, where I got a job with a travel agency where I remained for twenty years. At fifty-nine I was made redundant but worked on for a further five years with an oil company and an advertising agency – always as a telephone operator, the job I had learnt in the Services. In 1977 and now on my own, I decided to retire and married Arthur about two years later. He and his wife had been friends with us before he was widowed. Arthur was a Dunkirk veteran and a keen Legion supporter. We left London and retired to Worthing. When we moved to Devon to be close to my son and his family, we transferred to the Legion down there. I continued to attend meetings after Arthur died in 1994 and even now, as age marches on, I attend whenever I can in order to keep in touch.

Stuart Chislett

Fire Watcher, Home Guard, Bevin Boy, Royal Engineers. Sapper, Head Observer, Royal Observer Corps.

When war broke out I was thirteen and living in Epsom, Surrey. I joined the school fire watching team, patrolling the roof space during the air raids, checking for incendiary bombs. Although not in the direct line of fire, the London blitz of 1940-41 resulted in constant ack-ack activity with search lights, barrage balloons and shrapnel falling all around. During the Battle of Britain several German aircraft were shot down around Epsom Downs and gangs of us children would rush off on bicycles to find the scene of the crash. If we got there before the RAF police and recovery teams we could scrounge souvenirs.

By late 1941 things had quietened down and, still only fifteen and under age, I joined the Home Guard, unofficially of course but possibly because I was tall and useful as right marker for parades. The threat of airborne invasion by saboteurs was more to the fore and we were responsible for patrolling the wide open spaces of the Downs. We learned all the usual drills - shooting and platoon attack routines - under a 64 year old ex-regular Army Sergeant.

In March 1944 and my 18th birthday, I was expecting my Army call up, assuming that my Home Guard training would stand me in good stead. But fate took a dramatic twist as I was caught up in the dreaded ballot of our National Service Registration Card Numbers; those with a number ending with 0 or 9 were directed to work in an essential industry - at that time coal mining, the famous Bevin Boys, named after the Minister of Labour Ernest Bevin. For some reason the Government had not made mining a reserved occupation and a vast number of young colliers had joined up to take jobs in armament factories.

So it was that in late March 1944 I reported for training to the Prince of Wales Colliery,

Pontefract where we were paid the going rate for underground workers, £3 10 Shillings, (£3.50p), for a six hour shift. Then came the day that we were to go below and we were issued with safety helmet, steel capped boots, overalls, water bottle and safety lamp; the latter had the same number as a brass token. The lamp was handed in each day in exchange for the token and vice versa at the end of the shift, as a check that we were not still underground. Before descending we were checked for 'contraband' by way of matches, lighters or tobacco.

No Bevin Boy will forget the initiation drop in the cage to pit bottom. Coal was 'wound' very rapidly, at least 70 feet per second but almost half that speed for us. The gates clang open and the first impressions were of a dirty, dusty smell mixed with decaying matter - the product of rocks undisturbed for millennia, noisy machines and no toilet facilities, and although well lit around pit bottom there was not much light along the roads to the coal faces. The shaft was around 3,000 feet deep with working faces anything up to three miles from the pit bottom. Travel to the coal face was on trolleys along a 'road' that was in the main 8 feet high dropping to three or four feet at the face. Bevin Boys did only ancillary jobs involving haulage and some very boring periods standing at control points ready to stop any coal tub that had broken away or derailed.

Probably three or four colliers actually worked at the face operating the coal cutter, then depositing the coal on a conveyor to the main 'road', at this point we placed coal tubs and moved them for clamping to the main haulage cable to pit bottom. All coal that fell off had to be shovelled into the tubs. It was important that we painted a code number on a lump of coal to identify the production of each coal face; the tubs were weighed above ground and, as colliers were paid partly by results, our breaks were inclined to be short. There was an almost continuous creaking as the ground and rock settled; the colliers knew what all these sounds meant and if they ran we should run too! Luckily this never happened.

By early 1946 those miners who had served in the Forces were given early release if they returned to the pits and the Bevin Boys were given the option to volunteer for the forces. I opted for the forces and did six weeks 'square bashing' at Canterbury, and found myself in the Royal Engineers and subsequently posted to a Bomb Disposal Unit. This entailed clearing up duties with low priority unexploded bombs, in open country and beaches. The minefields laid in 1940 on all southern beaches were being cleared and many local authorities wanted their beaches back for the holiday season. The procedure was high pressure, lorry-mounted pumps moving along the beach, with water jets sweeping it ahead, from behind an armoured blade on the lorry. Most mines were uncovered and exploded by the pressure; a few defied destruction and were exploded with plastic explosives or rifle fire. This was a very tedious operation especially moving the hoses forward to keep the end in the sea when the tide was receding. Not much heroics but a lot of wet work and freezing in the winter.

I was 'demobbed 'in January 1948 having reached the rank of Corporal and joined the Royal Observer Corps in 1974, based in South Molton. The duties of the ROC at that time had changed very significantly from pure aircraft reporting to a much more sinister defence remit brought about by the 'Cold War' which necessitated underground locations. I retired in 1991, age 65, having reached the rank of Head Observer. My ROC service was the most enjoyable part of my time in uniform.

*****

Simon Clarke
Army. Army Air Corps. Sergeant.

I joined the TA first, back in 1988, aged seventeen when the only enemy the Army worried about was the big Russian bear. Then, in Jan 1990, I joined the Regular Army becoming Air Trooper Clarke in the Army Air Corps, completing my basic training and being posted to Middle Wallop for my trade training. As most soldiers can, I still remember through rose tinted glasses and with a peculiarly odd sense of humour, those days of training. All those early morning inspections, of sleeping on the floor next to my bed block so as not to mess it up, and all the rest of it.

I was posted to my first squadron that June and straight in to the Cold War readiness drills I went, deploying on exercise to colourful places like France and Belgium. Then came 2 Flight based at Netheravon in the middle of Salisbury Plain. Not that we were there much, mind you, for as part of the Allied Command Europe Mobile Force (AMF) we spent almost the whole year away from the UK. Starting the year in Norway with Arctic Training and then spending the remainder of the year bouncing around Europe – Portugal, Turkey, Cyprus and elsewhere, conducting multi-national exercises. After this I spent nine months with 8 Flight AAC, based at Stirling Lines, Hereford, supporting UK Special Forces, operating the Augusta 109 and doing some of the best white knuckle rides that money can't buy.

By 1994 I had been all over Europe and deployed to Canada and America. It was just as I imagined the remainder of my military career would be mapped out. Wrong! It was now that the Balkans began to raise its head. So, off I went under the banner of the United Nations, to a place called Ploce on the Dalmatian coast with a new fangled outfit known as 24 Airmobile Brigade: the marriage of an infantry battalion with an Army Air Corps Regiment – a strange fish out of water, so we were. The docks that made up our camp quickly became known as Ploce Death Camp. Almost weekly, and without fail, there would be a horrendous storm, our tents would be flattened and the land reclaimed from the sea would flood. I well remember standing up to my knees in water queuing at the cookhouse for our full English breakfast. How the chefs managed I don't know, but hats off to them.

Operational tours continued over the next few years to Bosnia, everywhere from Mostar in the south, to Banju Luka in the north and all points in between. Then, off the back of my last tour I was sent to Northern Ireland for a six month stint, spending my time between Aldergrove and Bessbrook Mill in South Armagh working as a door gunner in a Lynx Mk 7. I returned after this to what had become 16 Air Assault Brigade and went to work as a signaller, working within Battle Group HQ. It was during this relatively quiet time that I got married and attempted to settle down. But no, along came a nine month unaccompanied secondment to Belize to assist 25 Flight AAC and the jungle warfare school. It was only after this that I returned to Regimental life and, apart from the occasional trip to Canada, managed to enjoy a few years of relative peace and quiet.

Then, in 2003 the balloon went up again and I was off to Iraq, where we replaced those who had been on operations. Starting in Basra, we then moved north via the Garden of Eden with the Dutch, finally ending up in Alamara for the remainder of the tour. Here we operated close to the Iran-Iraq border, supporting and re-supplying our small patrol bases and isolated outposts. I returned from this and was posted to the School of Army Aviation to take up a teaching post. I really enjoyed passing on my knowledge to the next generation. It is an amazingly rewarding job taking a young man or woman and imbuing them with the knowledge and skills they will need for what lies ahead. I did this for three happy and well settled years. However, time flew and I found myself back with old friends - 663 Squadron AAC, now armed with the Apache and based at Wattisham.

Before I arrived even, I knew that the Squadron was soon to deploy to Afghanistan. Yet more family upheaval, so we decided to look around for somewhere permanent. Vanessa, my wife, is a North Devon lady born and bred, coming from Marwood just north of Barnstaple. We looked around here and there, eventually settling on South Molton, where we moved in December 2008. Not long afterwards I joined the South Molton branch of the RBL, mostly in anticipation of leaving the Army, in the knowledge that I would be able to remain in touch with Service people. In late 2008, I deployed to Afghanistan where we operated mainly out of MOB Bastion, as it was then known. The Apache worked in support of all Multinational ground forces, and we ranged all over the provinces of Helmand and Kandahar assisting with all types of operations. Then, in 2011, I was back again, still working with the Apache. After this I embarked upon what should be my final assignment: back to the Depot where I took up the post of Senior Instructor. This time I am working, not with recruits as before but helping to develop and mentor new instructors who were teaching for the first time. This has always been very rewarding on a personal level. I am due to remain here for the remaining eighteen months I have left to serve, taking me to twenty-four years of service.

*****

Lara Clisby-Brown
Womens Royal Naval Service, Steward. Able Rate.

I spent my childhood in Bishops Nympton, having moved down from Carterton, Oxford when I was small. I went to Bishops Nympton junior school then onto South Molton senior school and on to Bicton Collage to do an equitation course, as I intended to spend my life working with horses. I was working in a yard in Wootton Courtenay, Somerset, painting stables and thought there must be more to life that this, so off I went to the recruitment office in Barnstaple and joined the WRNS.

In February 1991 I joined *HMS Raleigh*, aged twenty-two, for my basic training, lots of marching, running, kit musters, polishing shoes and boots. I passed out in April 1991 and decided to become a steward as the Royal Navy Steward School was at the same location, and I remained there until April having passed all my exams with a 98.7% average. Being top of my class I could choose my next base and I decided to go to *HMS Dolphin*, Gosport, the Navy's main submarine base at that time. My uncle, who was a Royal Marine, recommended it as a good base as submariners were very laid back. And he was right. I had a good time at *Dolphin* where my main duties were looking after the officers in the wardroom. On arrival I worked in the silver store, cleaned an awful lot of silver and also worked in the wardroom bar. *Dolphin* was a lot of fun – yes, lots!

In October 1990 WRNS were allowed to serve at sea for the first time, and my first draft was *HMS Broadsword*, a Type 22 ASW, in September 1992. There were about 250 men and one mess deck of 18 WRNS. Life on board was very different from a shore base, I had a small locker for all my clothes, I was on the bottom bunk of a six bed golsh where it was difficult to sit up in bed without banging your head. In February 1993 we were sent to the former Yugoslavia to take part in Operation Grapple, patrolling the coast to uphold the arms embargo. It was not very exciting as we had to be in a constant state of readiness.

Whilst on station we did a lot of visiting to Italy, Spain, France and Greece. When alongside, our shifts enabled us to have plenty of free time. We had a very good Captain. Venice was lovely, I remember going out with the girls, finding the inevitable Irish bar, (whereever you go there's bound to be one), then off to a 'piano bar' (?) that you had to knock on the door to get in. We left at about 4 am and spent hours walking around Venice trying to find the ship. We arrived on board just in time to go to work. In July 1993 we had just handed over to our replacement ship when there was a fire in the main machinery space which took over 4 hours to control and all the hatches had to be closed to save the ship. We lost two crew. Regrettably they were shut down there with the fire. After that we just wanted to get home. Whilst on *Broadsword* we were lucky enough to go on exercise in the Norwegian Fjords which were amazing, together with the reindeer steaks sampled in Tromso, one of the most northerly cities in Norway.

In April 1994 I was drafted to RNAS Culdrose, Cornwall, home of the Search and Rescue helicopters together with Seahawks and Lynx. Whilst at Culdrose I took an opportunity to return to Norway for two months with the Royal Marines on their annual winter training. We flew out to Oslo in January 1995. It was an experience, like living in a Christmas card. I worked in the Sergeants' and Officers' mess, which was a very nice lakeside hotel. Together with a few other junior ranks we had a fab time. I did stay in a tent along with some other WRNS who were there, it was minus 21 degrees at night but we were sustained by lots of hot tea, and chocolate laced with whisky. I left Culdrose in May 1995 and joined *HMS Beaver*, another type 22 running from Plymouth. We were due to go to America and Canada but returned to the Adriatic to join a NATO task force with ships from America, Canada, France and Germany. We had a few runs ashore with the Americans. They are interesting. The Canadian ship used to do a very nice drink called Moose's Milk, which had a kick like a mule or was it a Moose? In November 1995, after a lot of thought I gave in my 18 months' notice. It was living on board that made up my mind. The girls joining the ships were all very young and thought that to be a good sailor you had to out drink the men, go ashore, return to the mess and make enough noise to wake the dead. Then get stroppy when you pulled them up the next day. I decided that this was not for me. I was discharged from *HMS Raleigh* in April 1997. Concerning WRNS serving at sea, I remember a comment of an officer from my first ship. He said he liked WRNS on board as they made the place look pretty. No comment necessary or required, thank you!

I moved back to Bishops Nympton and in June 1997 and got a job working for North Devon Council in the benefits department, and I am still there as I enjoy the job. I am now engaged to Andrew and live in a small village called Monkokehampton. I loved my time in the Navy and it has made me the person I am today, I have some good memories and good friends from my service.

*****

Andrew Coates
Son of Commander Gordon Coates. Royal Navy.

I was born in 1961, in Clive, Shropshire, and am the youngest of the family.
As my father was in the Navy, I was sent away to boarding school at the age of seven and went to Oundle School in Peterborough when I was thirteen. I left school and went on to university where I studied Modern Languages, including Welsh as I went to a Welsh University. I had decided to go into either the Navy or the Police but failed on both accounts due to poor eyesight. This meant I had to choose something else – panic! I went with the flow at the time which was gaining accountancy qualifications, so I struggled through a further four years of training to become an accountant.

I worked in the Channel Islands for a few years, in both Jersey and Guernsey, then came and worked in a large firm in London where I remained for a further twelve years. In 1994 I began work for a multinational company as finance director which meant travelling frequently to the Midlands although I was based here in Devon. When that company failed I decided to give the private sector a miss, so decided to go into Local Government where I am now, working for South Molton town council as Finance Officer and Deputy Town Clerk. Although never having served in HM Forces myself, my father served most of WWII in the Royal Navy and for many years afterwards, and I am proud to have been asked to give a short account of his career.

My Father, Gordon Coates, joined the Navy early in the war and went to Canada to train as a pilot. He flew Fairey Swordfish off various aircraft carriers back and forth across the Atlantic. Although reticent to talk of his time in the Navy, I knew he had survived numerous scrapes and adventures. On one particular occasion, having been lost at sea in thick fog and with his fuel gauge saying but one third remaining, Ireland was three hours away. Not possible to reach but to ditch was suicidal with the Swordfish's fixed undercarriage. So, they ditched everything they could…all their gear and ammo, and just kept flying. Fuel needle remained constant…another hour and still constant. But how? Impossible but true. Half an hour more and fuel level still constant. Quite unbelievable. Ireland now closing so he decided to get as close as possible and ditch. Eventually Ireland was below, fuel gauge suddenly read zero… engine spluttered and stopped. Floated down to crash-land in a bog between rocks. Landed and flipped over but safe…they were alive. Irish were very suspicious but helped them to right the aircraft…ladies stitched torn fabric with needles and thread. All was well and they got safely back on board. Impossible to explain and father called this story 'Wings of God'. And with some justification!

After the war he test flew in Ireland and in 1951 he was at *Daedalus*, flying Sea Otters for Search and Rescue and from there to Lossiemouth where he and Jock Anderson were the S and R team. After this he was posted to St Merryn as senior pilot of 796 Squadron which moved subsequently to Culdrose. He spent the remainder of his naval days in Air Traffic Control serving as SATCO on *HMS Hermes* and other appointments at several Air Stations. He retired in 1957 and lectured at S.G.Brown to foreign students on Naval Equipment, finally retiring to Exmoor in 1979.

Concluding on a personal note, I was delighted to have been asked by the Chairman of the South Molton Branch of the RBL to be their Secretary and, thus far, have thoroughly enjoyed being part of their team.

Fred Crowley
Royal Navy. Diver. Petty Officer Diving.

Born in 1942, I joined the Marine Engineering branch of the Royal Navy at the age of fifteen, at a time when Great Britain was a significant naval power. Our surface fleet was in excess of 250 vessels including 8 Aircraft Carriers, 9 Cruisers, 80 Destroyers and Frigates, 100 Minesweepers and Patrol Boats, and numerous maintenance vessels. There were nearly 50 submarines, and another 135 ships were being re-fitted or in reserve. Total manpower was in the region of 152,000. Sadly, today our navy is a fraction of what it used to be.

We had the Home Fleet based in various ports in the UK, in addition to The Mediterranean fleet, the South American/South Atlantic squadron and the Far East fleet based in Singapore and Hong Kong. In the UK there were significant numbers of training establishments, covering all the main maritime specialisations for a modern fighting force.

I started my training at the boys' establishment, *HMS Ganges*, near Ipswich. It lasted for one year and the main focus was on discipline and learning seamanship skills. Conditions were, to say the least, spartan. We lived in unheated wooden huts (messdecks), the food was terrible and the slightest infringement resulted in harsh punishment. Although flogging had been abolished in the 19th century, boys could be, and were flogged. The 'cat o nine tails' was not used, rather a six foot split bamboo cane. These were known as 'cuts', and boys were sentenced to 3, 6, 9, or 12 'cuts'. The shock of the punishment rendered some boys unconscious.

After this we went on to further training establishments, appropriate to our trades, before joining the Fleet. I was to spend about six months on my first ship, a destroyer which had seen service during WWII. Conditions were extremely cramped as about twenty men in our mess deck lived in a space about twice the size of a domestic lounge. We slept in hammocks that were quite comfortable. During the day they were lashed up and stowed in hammock nettings. The ship operated a 'canteen' messing procedure, whereby the crew prepared their food each day then took it to the galley to be cooked by the chef. Clothes were washed in buckets and dried in the boiler room. The highlight of most days was the rum issue, but at sixteen I had to wait another four years until I became entitled to 'draw my tot'.

My next ship was an aircraft carrier. I was astonished to find that the crew slept in bunks, and we had a dining hall – luxury! I spent eighteen months in this ship, all of it in foreign waters. It was deployed to a world cruise, but it was during this time that I realised that my ambition was to become a navy diver and on returning to the UK I applied for diver training.

The course was at Portsmouth and, upon arrival, the Chief Diver told me to report to his office in one hour. There he handed me a travel warrant to enable me to travel back to my ship. When I asked the reason for this, he explained that given my slight stature, and apparent lack of muscle, I would last no longer than a week. I was less than polite in declining his offer. Only five of us had passed out of a class of thirty and became qualified as a 'shallow water diver'. We used oxygen re-breather sets, but the equipment limited us to a depth of thirty feet. If we strayed any deeper we ran the risk of suffering from oxygen narcosis, a potentially life threatening condition. I came pretty close on a couple of occasions, due to the fact that we didn't actually have depth gauges.

My duties were mainly dealing with minor underwater ship repairs, and harbour searches. The most unpleasant of these were carried out in Hong Kong where we regularly recovered bodies which had fallen (or been pushed) from junks in Repulse Bay

After about nine months I was selected for further diver training and initially returned to the fleet diving section in Portsmouth. We were all interviewed by the Chief Diver, but this time he didn't offer me a travel warrant! This course introduced us to 'air' diving, and we used double air tanks which were known as SABA sets. Using this kit we could dive to a depth of 120 feet. It was a tough course with a failure rate of 70%. We learned various skills such as navigation and night diving. We normally operated a 'buddy' system which was two divers joined by a six foot rope. Occasionally we dived solo on a 180 foot lifeline. Communication with the dive tender was by way of signals on the lifeline called 'bells and pulls'.

Further courses took place in Scotland and Malta, and these included the use of other diving equipment, mine clearance, and endurance swimming. I spent about nine years as a diver, and although there were some 'hairy' moments, I thoroughly enjoyed myself and had some wonderful experiences. These included diving under the ice in the Arctic, with whales in Canadian waters, with giant mantas in the Indian Ocean, numerous dives in the Red Sea and the Great Barrier Reef. I learned to be wary of some types of shark, but generally I didn't mind being underwater with them. However, I hated sea snakes and spent some dives convinced that I was about to be bitten.

During my service I lost some good friends in various circumstances. The most tragic, was when the Indian cruiser Mysore rammed our destroyer *HMS Hogue* in the Indian Ocean, killing sixteen of the crew. However, we all accepted that this was part of life in the navy, and basically just got on with the job. Would I do it again? Too right I would.

*****

Robert Davison
42 Cdo Royal Marines. Corporal.

I was born in Rushden, Northamptonshire, in 1957, the one lad among four sisters (I joined up to get away from them all!). Father, a true Geordie, was a builder and mother worked from home as well as looking after us lot. The usual school days, I suppose, in and out of scrapes like everybody else, but I loved my sport, especially cross-country. I left school at sixteen having worked as a farm labourer and was then taken on in an ironmonger's shop. While at school I joined the Boys' Brigade – my first experience of discipline and uniform. I thought hard about the Marines from an early age but my father assured me that I would never make it. This only made me more determined than ever.

I began training at the RM Depot at Deal in Kent as a junior and finally got to passing out when an adult, due to being delayed by injuries on training. Next came CTCRM at Lympstone for selection and full commando training. All the usual hell and horrors, in particular that bloody six foot wall and all that doubling about the place; I am both short, and built more for endurance. Being a short a… meant the log runs weren't much fun either. Anyway, I survived it all and got posted to 42 Cdo RM at Bickleigh,

Plymouth. First memories were of breaking in somewhere and drinking illicit beer with a chum who was in the Recce Troop. A year or so later, in 1976, came Op Banner, Northern Ireland where we were posted to Andersonstown and where I was part of the CO's Rover Group. I returned safely but got sent back almost immediately for a second and shorter tour.

After this I decided to take up a trade as a Metal Smith (welding etc) which I did at Bordon with the REME. Success here entailed a move to the Commando Logistic Regiment (Cdo Log Regt) at Plymouth. Life here included Norway and the annual Arctic Warfare training. The survival side was no problem, fun in fact, but the skiing with bergens was not my cup of tea at all – I've never really hacked it. Work now for me became an annual trip to the Arctic, to deal with the repair and maintenance of the commando vehicles. And it was early one morning in April 1982 that I was warned off for the Falklands. Pressure and the pace of life grew ever more hectic. Later that month I flew out to Ascension Island where I boarded the Royal Fleet Auxiliary, *Sir Galahad.*

We sailed almost immediately and headed for Ajax Bay. On getting close we passed the grim spectacle of *HMS Antelope* which was on fire and sinking. As soon as we arrived we got ourselves ashore and set up camp. There was no ground opposition but we were attacked daily by the Argentinian Air Force using their Super Etendards with 1,000 lb bombs. The pilots were brave and good but, mercifully, not all their bombs exploded such as the one that came down but ten metres from me. The next closest, however, blew me off my feet and killed several of those nearby. One of our jobs there was to take control of the increasing numbers of Argentinian prisoners, searching them for weapons and grenades before handing them over to the Military Police. All in all it was a tough trip but we came away knowing that a good job had been done.

After the Falklands I joined 45 Cdo RM in Arbroath, Scotland and it was back to the Arctic Warfare routine. A couple of years here and it was down south to join RM Poole where I did two years in support of the Special Boat Service (SBS). This took me up to 1990 when I rejoined the Cdo Log Regt and, guess what, it was back to Arctic Warfare! My next operational tour, however, was Op Haven in 1992 when we were sent out to southern Turkey on a humanitarian operation, looking after Kurdish refugees who had come across the border from northern Iraq. This entailed both armed foot and vehicle patrol, but in the main we were involved in looking after the refugees themselves.

Following on from this came two tours to Afghanistan. On the first (Op Herrick 5) in 2006, we were based in Kandahar and my work took me back to my trade as a metal smith, servicing the vehicles. Although not on the front line we were mortared fairly frequently. Sadly, 3 Cdo Brigade, who we were supporting, took several casualties, including a number of fatalities. I returned a couple of years later where, by this time, the workshops had moved to Camp Bastion. Conditions had improved immeasurably with all sorts of goodies available and, don't tell anyone this, we even had the luxury of air conditioning. My time here was again spent in the workshop, on this occasion repairing multi-lift vehicles that had been knackered, they had been worked literally down to their axles.

This was my last operational tour but by this time I had completed my 22 years of adult service and was on the Long Service List. By this time I had moved up to the RM Base at Chivenor in North Devon which was the new home of the Cdo Log Regt. I finally left the Service on 31st July 2012. I had been living in South Molton since 2005 and just before leaving the Marines I joined the South Molton Branch of the RBL, which I greatly enjoy.

*****

Charles Day
Royal Navy. Able Seaman.

I was born in Deptford, London, in 1936, the baby in a family of four youngsters. Dad was a bricklayer, attached to the RAF during WWII, and Mum worked at the Royal Arsenal, Woolwich. My first memories of life were of the barrage balloons and the wailing sirens during the blitz. It was fun for a youngster and we would go hunting for bits of shrapnel when the raid was over, sometimes still hot to the touch. We were bombed pretty badly but life in the Anderson shelter was an adventure, too. We had one lucky escape, however, when our church, just a hundred yards away received a direct hit by a landmine and was totally destroyed. We moved out of London for a while, to Raunds in Northamptonshire, returning back to the 'smoke' after the war. I managed to get into the Roan's Grammar School. Good fun, it was, but I had to run the gauntlet in my smart uniform through some pretty mean streets and took a bit of stick.

I left at sixteen and went to work in the City at Lloyds, in Marine insurance.

I remember preparing myself for the inevitable National Service then going away for a holiday. On return the dreaded envelope was on the mat. My destination was Victoria Barracks, Pompey and I had to report between 10am and 4 pm. The trains were late and I only just made it whereupon the Master at Arms, who had wanted to get away early that day, introduced himself to me, living up to his nickname of 'Screaming Skull'. There followed the usual sharp introduction to the niceties of basic training – square bashing at a high rate of knots, starvation (never enough grub), bromide in the tea and the delights of washing, sewing and ironing. On one occasion, the camp tailor had us out on the square with our best uniforms on, inside out, standing with legs and arms apart looking like scarecrows, as he walked up and down the line chalking up the baggy bits for tailoring.

Then came the posting and I was off to Portland to join *HMS Ocean* (a light carrier of 22,000 tons) which carried Fairey Gannets and Sea Fires (RN version of Spitfires) armed with anti-submarine cannon. I was rated as OD (Ordinary Deckhand – the lowest form of life). Home was my hammock at the far end of the hangar along with fifty others. Life was certainly not private for it was here that we ate, slept, washed and shaved, and tried to relax – some hope of that with the watches constantly changing. A week later we sailed for Gib and the Med where we called in at Oran, Tangier, and, on the way back, Corunna, of Sir John Moore fame. We then hit a monstrous Force 12 hurricane out in the Bay of Biscay – not recommended for the faint hearted. Waves of fifty feet or more battered us all the way home where, at Portland, it was impossible to see the breakwater. We survived, just, but couldn't make the harbour and had to settle for standing off in Weymouth Bay. A fine welcome home for my first Christmas leave!

I was next posted as a relief on to a tiny nondescript, wooden minesweeper whose name escapes me. Our task was to look for unexploded WWII mines, which still littered the Dorset coastline. We found two, one of which was a dummy but the other I exploded with our bren gun after we had run out of Bofor's ammunition. So close were we to the mine that chunks of shrapnel embedded themselves in the superstructure and decking. Only here for a short time, my next posting was to Chatham and *HMS Tumult* (an anti-submarine frigate) armed with twin 4" guns and depth charges. By now the Cold War was at its height and our task was to patrol the Channel looking for inquisitive Soviet submarines. Much of our work was carried out in conjunction with *HMS Osprey* the onshore underwater establishment.

After this I transferred to *HMS Tyrian*, the same class as *Tumult*. Here I was Quartermaster, in charge of the gangway and of everything that came and went, up and down. We were, at that time, part of No 2 Anti-Submarine Squadron, whose Captain – known to all as Captain 'D' – was, as far as we were concerned, a particularly awkward individual, who took it upon himself to make surprise visits and turn the place upside down. He selected us just as we were setting off to patrol under the flight path of HM The Queen when she flew to Holland. Mercifully, we had foul weather all the way and Captain 'D', severely afflicted by 'mal de mer' was conspicuous by his absence throughout. Hurrah!

I saw out my time on *HMS Tyrian* and on return to Chatham was paid off. I only just managed to escape because the Suez crisis had blown up and most hands were retained. But I made it, and so ended my illustrious naval career whereupon it was back to the City and my old job. Not for long, however, as I just couldn't take it and decided on a complete life change when I was offered the job as a groundsman. I loved it, being back in the open air, and spent the rest of my working life out in the open working at one establishment or another. On retirement we moved down to the Westcountry where I enjoy my time shooting and fishing. And it was here, in 2006, that I joined the South Molton Branch of the RBL.

*****

Jeremy Dunn
Army. Royal Engineers. Sapper.

Born in November 1952, I joined the Army in July 1971. I trained first at Southwood Camp near Farnborough, which was built by Canadian Engineers back in WWII – and it felt like it. The barracks were thirty year-old wooden 'Spider' huts, the six legs of which were where we slept, the centre block being taken up by our distinctly spartan ablution facilities. The cookhouse was a simple galvanised iron shed and the food, not surprisingly, wasn't brilliant. I can well recall occasions when the dish on offer was spiced with the corpses of unfortunate cockroaches that had slipped from the ceiling above.

Training was hard yet enjoyable and our instructors tough and, in the main, fair. One exception was a brute who took us for watermanship training and who used to stand in the back of the assault boat while ordering us into the water to pull him in. We obeyed but one evening, having had enough and once in the water, tugged the boat sharply, watching with grim satisfaction as he disappeared straight over the back. Retaliation was swift and, on the next occasion, we were made to swim for it. Changing parades were hard, the worst being from No 2 Dress down to mess tin order, when we, by now totally naked, were marched about with one mess tin providing modesty to the fore and the other behind.

I left Southwood that November having passed off the square and joined 32 Field Squadron at Ripon in Yorkshire. Our primary role here was Harrier support (keeping their small airfields in shape). While there I saw service in BAOR, Sudan, Cyprus, Belize and undertook my first operational tour in Northern Ireland. Operation Mirza was a three month tour in Southern Sudan and was classified as a Development Aid Project. This was in 1974, the year after the Yom Kippur war. Because of fuel shortages and the recent conflict, we flew out in a Hercules C130, taking three days to reach our destination via Cyprus, Masirah, Nairobi and finally Wau in Sudan. The last leg was by Russian helicopter from Wau to Tonj. These machines, basic in the extreme, were so heavy they needed a runway to take off.

Operation Mirza was really the result of President Nimeiri looking to the West for help rather than towards communist Russia. He had, allegedly, kicked out his Russian advisers. Our task here was to upgrade two bridges over the River Tonj. We had to remove all the old concrete road decking and reinforce the piers and abutments before laying a wider concrete road deck. Each huge pour of concrete had to be worked on immediately. So, once the pour started there was no stopping. Nine hours a day of this in more than one hundred and twenty degrees was something of a challenge.

For R&R we had a few days in Khartoum. One of our favourite haunts was the Sudan Club, which was frequented by a varied mix of characters including Australian crop dusters, airline pilots, cabin staff, assorted expats – and us Sappers. Back at camp relaxation came in the shape of films, which were projected onto sheets sewn together and strung between two scaffolding poles. We watched from one side (the right way round) while local Dinka tribesmen watched from behind the screen and gazed uncomprehendingly at it all in reverse. Toilet facilities were in the shape of the dreaded Deep Trench Latrines (DTLs), where the occupant sat on a hole cut into planks of wood, perched precariously high above the unspeakable morass below. The lids were kept tight shut but, when opened for use, the insect world rose to greet the nether regions of he who sat above. Not for the squeamish. Supplies came in by Andover and a Sudanese Airways Russian 'Antonov' transport, the latter flown by Ukranians as suitably qualified Sudanese were hard to come by. Strange really that, at the height of the Cold War, we Brits were being re-supplied by personnel from the USSR.

In 1976 I did a tour in Belize when we were based at Airport Camp in the Harrier support role. An interesting tour as we could go snorkelling on the marvellous Belize Barrier Reef – the second largest in the world. We could also explore the interior where there were some of the finest Mayan civilisation ruins. But hurricanes there were, too, as the wreck of a ship stranded miles inland was clear proof. After this came

Germany and a posting to 2 Armoured Division Engineer Regiment at Osnabruck. Here Sapper Dunn took command of either an armoured personnel carrier or a tracked Spartan recce vehicle. While here I did my second operational tour in Ulster, the highlight, as I remember, being to sweep and search the grounds of Coleraine University prior to a visit by The Queen. Fingers were crossed and prayers offered that we had missed nothing!

My final posting, in 1981, was to Long Marston where we maintained flexible barges and pillow tanks for bringing petroleum products ashore. A sudden and unexpected task here was when the Falklands war started and we had to prepare a lot of kit for the South Atlantic. Sadly much of it went down with the Atlantic Conveyor. In 1983 I left the Army and returned to my roots in North Devon. I am now happily married with two wonderful children. Apart from my family, I also enjoy country pursuits and am an active Sunday Church bell ringer. I also take a close interest in my village of North Molton and I am a member of the local Parish Council and the local History Society. I have been a member of the South Molton Branch of the RBL for nine years.

*****

George Gallagher
Army. National Service. Private.

I was born in the London Borough of Kensington in 1930 and I spent most of my school days living in Harrow, Middlesex.

I was nine years old when the Second World War started, and most of my school time was spent in air raid shelters. I left school when I was 14 years old and my Dad told me that I could become an apprentice bricklayer or a carpenter and joiner. I chose carpenter and joiner but I could not start until I was 15 years old. So for the first year I worked making flush doors and ladders. The sirens were still calling us to the shelters for protection from the V2 rockets that were regularly coming over.

When I was 20 I got my 'call up' for National Service and I had to report to the Royal Army Medical Corps, (RAMC), Queen Elizabeth Barracks, Crookham, Aldershot, Hants, to train as a Nursing Orderly. The first two weeks was training to become a soldier and then to be a Nursing Orderly. I was posted to Iserlohn, Germany, stationed at the army hospital. I was in the RAMC for 5 months.

On 12 April, 1951, I was transferred to the Queens Royal Regiment to train as a foot soldier in the infantry, at Sennelagar Deserted village. I was quite pleased to move because I didn't go much on bedpans and stuff like that. Must tell you about the time I had to carry the Bren gun. There we were out on manoeuvres, training very hard, running like mad through the woods, wearing our waterproof capes, the ones that made a two man tent, they have a point at the front and at the back. I was running like a madman when we came to this wide stream, and you had to jump. Well, I did but landed right in the middle, because I got my legs caught in the cape. It was then that I heard the sergeant screaming at the top of his voice. "You horrible little man, you are not fit to carry a gun like that!" He came at me like a mad bull, screaming, arms and legs going all ways. He jumped in the water and snatched the gun out of my hand and gave it to another poor soul.

The next thing that happened was they wanted 800 men to form the First Battalion of the Royal Norfolk Regiment to go to the Korean War and I was one of them. We had no time to think that we were going to fight; we just did as we were told. So back to England to do some hard training: and I can tell you that this was for real! It was so hard that it did not do my feet any good and at the end they said I would not last the Korean winter. Some of my mates went but I never heard from them again or what might have happened to them. As it was National Servicemen who were going to fight I think that it was hushed up from the public. In the end I got an early discharge from the Army. I left in October, 1951. My service with the colours was 348 days and three different cap badges!

To those National Service men who went to the other sides of the world and to those who never came back, they are my heroes. We should never forget them. I enjoy the friendship of the Royal British Legion meetings with many chaps of different ages and experiences. It's nice to have a good humoured and friendly chat and I enjoy the various presentations that are arranged.

22429813, Private G Gallagher Sir!

Paul Hackman
Army. Royal Wessex Yeomanry, 6 Rifles. Sergeant.

I was born in Barnstaple in 1982 to Bob and Ruth Hackman. I grew up in the small rural hamlet of Ash Mill, set deep in the idyllic countryside of North Devon, and attended the local schools. It was during this period that I joined the Air Training Corps at No 1146 Squadron in Barnstaple. Life here was fun including mock aerial dog fights in Bulldog single wing aircraft, and glider training at Chivenor and RAF St Mawgan in Cornwall. Not surprisingly my heart was first set on a career with the RAF but I found that manoeuvres on the ground – field exercises and camps – were even more to my liking and came naturally to my country background.

After leaving school I remained at home for a while, earning money in the countryside by helping local gamekeepers and beating on private shoots. I then worked for my father in the family building business, but it was not long before I was tempted to go along to the local TA Centre in Barnstaple – 'D' Squadron, The Royal Wessex Yeomanry. I joined the TA aged nineteen, encouraged by news filtering back from the Iraq war. It was, I thought to myself, high time to get in there and see a bit of the action myself. I got through basic training as quickly as possible, really enjoying anything to do with the outdoors, plus the warm and friendly comradeship I found. My first job on joining the squadron was as a driver/signaller, before I undertook a second course as a gunner/loader on the Challenger 2 tank. I completed this at the Royal Armoured Corps Centre at Bovington in Dorset.

With all this under my belt, it was not long before I heard word that volunteers were being sought to join the Regular regiment – The Royal Dragoon Guards Battle Group – for Operation Telic 5 in Iraq. This entailed the regiment being broken down into one armoured squadron and three others operating in the dismounted role. I immediately volunteered and in July 2004 found myself posted to the regiment in Munster, Germany. Here I joined 'B' Squadron for the three months before they deployed.

Once in Iraq, I found myself in Basra as part of a large patrol operating either on our feet or on mounted escort duties. Apart from desultory mortaring of our camp when, as far as I could tell, the only place to get taken out was the Burger Bar, we were not unduly disturbed. Our first major contact came when our vehicle patrol was escorting a convoy to Al Amarah. We were ambushed and a brisk fire fight took place where we accounted for a number of enemy killed.

Soon after this I volunteered to be bodyguard to the ATO (Ammunition Technical Officer, known by everyone simply as 'Bomb Disposal'). I thoroughly enjoyed this highly complex and often quite hairy work, and remained in this post for the remainder of our tour. Life varied: sometimes it was peace and quiet while we waited, on other occasions it was frantic activity on the front line for hours on end. I very soon learned to hold these quite exceptional men and women in the highest regard where, under extreme pressure and often in mortal danger, they were somehow able to remain cool, calm and collected. Remarkable people, I can assure you, their courage was quite inspirational and they were, and remain today, universally admired.

My own particular task was to protect the ATO as closely as possible and I remember vividly when we were called forward to where the suicide bombers had been only partially successful. The instability of the remaining explosives, now dangerously exposed and sometimes still smoking, and the ghastly body parts and human entrails of the bombers, either entangled in the remains of some vehicle or scattered far and wide, are something that I will never be able to forget.

Since coming home, I have concentrated on my TA career and I am now a Troop Leader in the rank of Sergeant. I thoroughly enjoy my time with the RBL where I have made a number of good friends. In particular I have the highest regard for the oldest of our members who went through so much during WWII, and of whom we still have six in the branch. In 2011 and 2012, I was a member of the South Molton Branch team that competed in the RBL thirty mile speed march across Exmoor. It was an event we won handsomely on both occasions as well as collecting the prize for raising the most money for the Legion.

My immediate ambition is to serve a full tour of duty on Op Herrick in Afghanistan before the operational side of soldiering is drawn to a close. Time, I know, might just be against me, but we'll have to see.

Nigel Hills
Army. Royal Military Police. Corporal.

Born in 1936, I left school at seventeen and a half and aimed for a career in the Police, I knew National Service was on its way, so I worked in the Co-op Bakery, and waited. Eventually call-up came and I made my preferred choice of units. My interviewer asked me why I wished to join my County Regiment. I did not. Rather I had put RMP, followed by RMP and then the Royal Berkshire Regiment.

'Military Police are all regular soldiers', he told me – a blatant lie as I later discovered, but it resulted in my signing on for the three/four years Regular Engagement. After four and a half months at Inkerman Barracks, Woking where, each fortnight, about one hundred men began their training, the surviving 'Probationers' passed out as fledgling Lance Corporals. Then, after two weeks of embarkation leave, and on returning to Woking, we were enlightened as to our various destinations. Those of us for BAOR left shortly for Harwich and the boat to Ostend, then by rail to Krefeld. Here we were given a list of postings to the various Provost companies throughout Germany and Austria, and but ten minutes to decide our preferences. And so it was that I arrived at Gibralter Barracks, Verden – 7th Armoured Division Provost Coy.

Early days were spent acclimatizing to our new surroundings, and having our hopelessly ill-fitting uniforms tailored to fit properly and unit flashes – the Desert Rats – sewn on. We were allocated to Sections – 1 Sergeant, 2 Corporals and 13 Lance Corporals – within the Company, but were rarely up to strength. Most Provost Companies had 'Out' Sections in the various garrisons which were completely self-contained and came with a cook. Ours were at Luneberg, Celle, Hohne and Soltau. Duties varied from security to mobile and foot patrols. When not on duty as such, each section had its own motor transport and stores to maintain. Those of us without driving licenses either gained instruction, or taught themselves on the Ford Willys jeeps and BSA motorcycles.

I was helped to learn German by local interpreters who were attached to all Provost units. At this time BAOR remained an Occupation Zone with a curfew from 2359 hrs where troops had to sign in and out of barracks. Provost patrols regularly checked pubs and bars, most of which remained open until much later, as well as the numerous 'Out of Bounds' areas. Early in 1955 I was posted to Luneberg Section, where the War Department had, in its wisdom, co-located within one Brigade, the Cameron Highlanders, the Irish Hussars and the Royal West Kent Regiment. That was fun! We were quartered in a large private property on the edge of town with individual accommodation and excellent messing facilities. It was the house where Himmler committed suicide after capture in 1945.

Our detachment was never up to strength and, with the large number of troops, we were always busy. Nevertheless we found time occasionally to host small functions. On one such, for the local German Police, a well-oiled guest remarked how authentic the town and village signs were on the Mess walls. No one enlightened him that they had all been 'borrowed' from nearby localities. Perhaps he would have found this surprising. Our Luneberg patch was eventually handed over to another Division and we returned to Verden. I next spent a period in the Investigation Department, was promoted and posted on to the Celle Section, which included a large RAF air base. Joint patrols with the RAF Police took place regularly, and an excellent working and social relationship was developed.

Training exercises were part and parcel of BAOR life – sometimes small and localized, on other occasions they involved long distances and lasted for several days. Route signing for convoys, setting up vehicle Harbour Areas and manning Information Posts were duties regularly undertaken. Very often the evenings involved little so, not infrequently, we would liberate a jeep and find ourselves a pub, well away from prying eyes. A vehicle work ticket stating 'Police Duties' covered a multitude of sins and was rarely checked. Once two of us accompanied a Royal Signals unit through the American zone and up to the East Germany border. Arriving at the designated area I enquired at a small farmhouse if we could sleep in the barn. The occupant asked us if we were Belgian or Dutch. On learning that we were British, she exclaimed 'English Tommies!' and invited us in, insisting that we sleep in the house. The barn was left to the Royal Signals subaltern and his Signalers.

When Conqueror tanks replaced Centurions, the multitude of bridges on the roads we would use in war had to be checked. This entailed a loaded Antar transporter physically traveling the routes. The Provost provided escorts for these enormous loads, plus jeeps with bi-lingual Warning Notices to front and rear, and motorcycle outriders. More than one German HGV driver lived to regret the day he ignored our warnings to steer clear, and had the off side of his vehicle sliced off by a Conqueror tank track. Celle, close to the extensive NATO ranges, was regularly visited by troops of the US, Canadian, Dutch, Belgian and the new German armies. Few problems occurred but we did once have to investigate how, allegedly, the mascot of a US Army formation – a bison – turned overnight into tins of bully beef. But no, false alarm, it reappeared safe and sound, as mysteriously as it had vanished!

Spring 1957 saw me returning to Woking for demob. On eventually moving to Devon and with no localized RMP Association branch, the RBL in South Molton seemed to be the natural alternative choice.

*****

Joe Hoar
Army. Royal Wessex Yeomanry. Lance Corporal.

I was born in Barnstaple in 1989, remarkably the seventh son of John and Jacqui Hoar. I was brought up in the small market town of South Molton where I was educated at the local schools. No academic by any stretch of the imagination, I infinitely preferred the active, outdoor life where I competed in the Ten Tors expedition, acted as 'hare' to the local pack of Bloodhounds, and did well at tennis and cricket where I played for local teams. It was, I freely admit, a wonderfully happy childhood which I and my large family enjoyed to the full.

Further education looked to me like being somewhat problematical and, although I completed my 'A' levels, I joined the TA at the earliest opportunity when I was barely seventeen. My first short tour away from home was to complete my Basic Training at Bassingbourn in Cambridgeshire. Initially military discipline came as something of a shock but, and to think of it makes me chuckle, I soon learned to play the game successfully. It was while completing my last year at college that I heard that the TA was looking for volunteers for Operation Herrick 12 in Afghanistan, in particular for those who might wish to work in Intelligence. At the same time I was offered a place at university, a small matter I had no hesitation on putting 'on hold' for the time being. I volunteered immediately and was accepted, pending my being successful on the preparatory courses. These came along thick and fast including a radio operators' course at the Royal Armoured Corps Centre at Bovington, followed by further assessments at Chilwell, after which it was back to Bovington for a Team Medic course.

In May 2010, I together with a number of other volunteers, was deployed to join my unit – 5 Regiment Royal Artillery – in Camp Bastion 2. I did not remain long in this backwater but was deployed forward to PB (Patrol Base) Three at Nahri Sarraj where I worked within the Intelligence Cell. Small arms attacks on the base were spasmodic, however the base suffered a number of battlefield casualties. Patrols into the local area were frequent but mostly inconsequential; however I well remember several sightings of the elusive Taliban and, on one particular occasion, benefiting from the close support of Apache helicopters when we were under attack. Another vivid but more sombre memory for me was when a close friend and two others were killed by a rogue Afghan soldier.

A while later I was posted across to the Mercian Regiment at Rahim Kalay on the edge of what is known as the Green Zone. Again I found myself working at the task of Intelligence gathering, and here patrolling was more frequent with numerous contacts when small arms and RPGs were used effectively against both us and our camp. A number of inter-regimental postings for this intrepid volunteer soldier came one after the other in rapid succession, culminating in my final posting to the Royal Regiment of Scotland (the old Argyll and Sutherland Highlanders) where I found myself still tied to the same job. My tour came to an end in November 2010.

Looking back on my time in Afghanistan, I freely admit to having learned an enormous amount about life and people in a very short space of time, but where I made some wonderful friends. I joined the RBL in early 2011 and thoroughly enjoy the camaraderie and fund raising activities. Almost before the ink was dry on my Application Form, I found myself swept into the Branch team for the arduous thirty-mile RBL speed march across the wild heights of Exmoor where the total climb was over three thousand feet and where each of us had to carry thirty pounds of kit. Our team won, I am proud to say. Not only the speed march itself but we gained a further award for raising the most money for the charity. I am now engaged in a university degree course at Worcester where I am studying to be a paramedic. Where this will take me eventually remains to be seen, but I am keen to remain in the Legion which I much enjoy.

Andy Horsnell
Army. Royal Artillery. Bombardier.

I was born in 1966 at Hampton, Middlesex, right next door to Hampton Court Palace, you understand, and the youngest of five. Dad was a chauffeur and when I was just two we followed him down to Southampton. I seem to have spent most of my childhood fighting my corner against my aggressive elders, least that's what I remember. I was a pretty average school kid but very sporty, running cross country and playing cricket and rugby for the school. First thoughts of Service life was for the RAF but, when my brother was rejected through colour blindness, I turned towards the Army. Beginning with a spell in the ACF, I applied for and was accepted for the Junior Leaders while still at school. I was rarin' to go…just couldn't wait.

Put on the train to Nuneaton, I was collected and taken into Bramcote. Once the gates had shut behind me, my feet didn't touch the ground for the whole of that year. Against advice, I got into the band as a trumpeter, our engagements included the 1983 Edinburgh Tattoo. I did cross country and the half marathon for the Regiment and found myself in the shooting VIII. After Passing Out came the posting, and for me it was to 32 Guided Weapons Regt in Bulford – yes, Salisbury Plain. Our main weapon was the Blowpipe (shoulder fired anti-aircraft missile), tasked to protect RAF missile sites. We then became part of the Allied Command Europe (ACE) mobile force and did six months of Arctic Warfare training, which included live missile firing. Volunteers were then called forward to join 2 Scots Guards on exercise in Washington State, USA – I went. No missiles here, I was simply a squaddie in a rifle platoon and loved it – a great adventure, very hard work and we got very fit. In fact they asked me to consider transferring but I was happy enough where I was.

After returning home my Battery (43 Bty) was sent to Cyprus. We were in support of the UN contingent who were peacekeeping along the Greek/Turkish Demarcation Line. Something of a holiday number, really, we managed to get in a lot of Adventure

Training in between work, including skiing and water skiing (you can do both in the same day in Cyprus), and rock climbing. Not to be missed, however, was the Limassol wine festival. Bloody fantastic, but don't ask me any more about it! On returning home I switched batteries to 21 Bty and was sent to Thorney Island as part of 26 Field Regt. From here came Op Banner (Northern Ireland) where it was to be our lot to guard HM Prison, Long Kesh (the infamous Maze). A pretty grim tour which entailed four days of guard duties at the Maze, followed by four days rural patrolling and then four days in Belfast in support of 40 Cdo, RM at North Howard Street Mill. Although the main campaign was waning we still got a lot of punishment shootings (knee and elbow cappings), some very aggressive provocation and the occasional shooting. At this time the RUC – very brave men – were being targeted by the IRA and we lost four during our time there.

Back home again we changed our Blowpipes for the more modern and powerful Javelin. Iraq was now at war with Iran and the Royal Navy's task was to keep open the Straits of Hormuz in order to keep the oil flowing. We were posted on board ships and, after training at *HMS Raleigh* and *HMS Phoenix*, I was posted to *HMS Gloucester* (a Type 42 Destroyer) for a six month's stint in the Gulf. Our action station on board was on the Heli Flight Deck and my crew was to fire the first ever Javelin from a British warship. No Iranians or Iraqis to play with though, they were too busy with each other. Home once more and we were off on another UN mission, this time to Bosnia. Our task here was to keep the warring factions – mainly the Croats and Serbs – apart. This we managed to do, but very often this resulted in them having a go at us, sometimes both at the same time. Mainly sniping which we could put up with, it was the atrocities that hit us the hardest. We would quite often come across a grisly massacre when whole families of civilians, men, women and kids, had been either shot or butchered and then partially burned and hidden. Sickening sights indeed, truly horrible examples of man's inhumanity to man, something that I have never been able to forget.

After this tour I had had enough. Earlier I had intended to transfer to the Army Physical Training Corps but a severe motor accident had put paid to that and, on walking out of the gates at Thorney Island, I became a civvy. My brother was running a business in North Devon and was looking for a new partner so I moved down to a small village just outside South Molton where he was set up. I had, in fact, joined the RBL while still in the Army but, after a short time with the Riders' Branch, had allowed it to lapse. I blew the dust off my membership in 2010 and joined the South Molton Branch. It's terrific. I thoroughly enjoy it, in particular meeting and chatting to other old sweats for which there never seems to be enough time. Last year I was a member (the oldest) of their victorious Exmoor 3030 team.

Spike Howells
Royal Air Force. Meteorological Branch. Flight Lieutenant.

As a child, I recall watching the Festival of Remembrance and learning about the Chelsea Pensioners marching proudly in their scarlet coats - veterans of the Boer and Great War. I longed to be part of the military, particularly, to fly.

Born in 1963, I grew up in northern England spending my formative years living close to a wartime airfield. I began gliding here, experiencing the thrill of flying – I can still close my eyes and imagine that airfield up-side-down above me! At eighteen, I began a career in meteorology, joining the Met Office as an Observer and working my way up to be a specialist military forecaster. I was fortunate to serve on many now defunct airfields like St Mawgan, Scampton, Brawdy, Cottesmore, Chivenor, Ascension Island & Laarbruch.

The role of the 'Met Man' on an airfield is to provide advice to aircrew to complete their task, be it low level attack, air-air refuelling, recce or close air support of troops and each has its weather limitations. Being interested in flying, I interacted with aircrew asking questions about their job. I attended squadron dining-in nights, becoming involved in 'japeish' behaviour. On one occasion, an emergency inflatable dinghy had been 'procured' and fixed beneath the cloth along the leading edge of the top table. Just as the speeches began, the auto-inflate cord was pulled and the top table's leading edge reared up spilling candlesticks & cutlery into the laps of senior officers. Such evenings ended with firing a mess cannon or practicing carrier landings on tables in the bar!

In the late 1980s, the RAF recruited forecasters to deploy with squadrons on operations and so I found myself joining the Mobile Met Unit undergoing Initial Officer Training at RAF Cranwell which was hard with regular inspections and leadership exercises. Today, when visiting, I still hear the ghostly sound of our

Drill Sergeant's boots clicking across the parade ground and anticipating his yell, "Stand still!"

January 1991 saw the start of the Gulf War and Iraq experiencing its worst winter in decades with Tornado crews attacking heavily defended Iraqi airfields in very marginal conditions. Just as this war ended, another started in the Balkans. Ultimately, our deployments to Iraq and the Balkans went on for longer than WW2, with our small unit of forty covering seven overseas bases in Bosnia, Croatia, Kosovo, Turkey, Kuwait and Italy. Each winter there was the annual exercise in Norway with compulsory attendance on an Arctic Survival Course – a week on a Norwegian mountain in January with temperatures of minus 18 C and 20 KT winds! We spent two nights in a tent, two in an igloo and one in a snow-hole all of which we constructed ourselves during the day (The snow hole was the least cold). Luckily, our kit and rations were excellent. Those who passed went on the exercise which meant living eight to a tent on Evenes airbase 400 miles north of the Arctic Circle in February. The days were short but the northern lights were stunning.

The detachments I particularly enjoyed involved deploying with a fast jet squadron and I was fortunate to do this with Harrier and Tornado squadrons. "Happy" 4 Sqn as they were known were a particularly sociable Harrier squadron. During the day, I supported their operations over Bosnia, during the evening it was beer and pizza.

Weather affects almost every aspect of military operations on land, sea and air, aircraft being particularly susceptible. Despite manufacturer's claims to be 'all-weather,' there are weather limitations on the aircraft, pilot, weapons and targeting systems. We aimed to assist at each level, for example, whilst based at Ali Al Salem Airbase in Kuwait in 1999, attacks on Iraqi missile systems often took place at dawn when light levels are poor. Thus we advised the best time to attack to avoid so called thermal cross-over – a metal anti-aircraft system in woods, during the night becomes colder than the surroundings, during the day it becomes hotter. There must, therefore, be a period around dawn and dusk when the system and the woods are the same temperature and so cannot be distinguished using infra red. It therefore cannot be targeted and so I would recommend a different attack time.

I had enormous fun in 'the mob' and peaked as a NATO Tactical Evaluator. But family life suffers as a result of long, frequent separation. I now teach cadets to fly and am Chief Flying Instructor on an RAF Training squadron. Much of my flying involves standardising squadron pilots but I also send cadet's solo, and I am rewarded by a 16 year-olds grin having just landed after their first solo flight - too young to drink or drive but they can fly an aeroplane! Their sense of achievement is massive and good to see.

I did my bit but the elders of our Branch and in particular the era that fought WW2 are my heroes and I salute them.

Keith Hurst
Royal Navy. Submarine Service. Petty Officer Electrician.

I was born in Battersea in 1932, into a Service family, my father having been in the Fleet Air Arm during WWII, and my grandfather for twenty-three years in the Navy before that (WWI). First real memories of life were of the Blitz and how much I enjoyed it, there being no school for weeks on end, and the thrill of watching the nearby anti-aircraft guns in action. Eventually, however, our house was bombed, me and my family surviving in the Anderson shelter in the garden. After the raid was over, we had to force the door open as it had been blocked by rubble and debris. Later, during the V1 and V2 offensive, I was evacuated to Rock in Cornwall when I and the others travelled by train into a new life with labels around our necks and with our one small suitcase each. Evacuee life, as I remember, was fun as we lived in a privileged home, run by the housekeeper to the Princes Bira and Chula of Siam. It was close to the beach and where, somehow, we had access to the magic of ice cream!

After the war, I returned to London and continued with school until I was fourteen, whereupon I took up an apprenticeship with an electrical firm. But life was not good – I found that I was being asked to do a man's job for a boy's wage (£2 per week) so I 'retired', took myself off to Trafalgar Square and joined the Navy. *HMS Royal Arthur* at Corsham came first where I undertook basic training – the usual brutal introduction to Service life, as I remember. From there I was sent to *HMS Collingwood* for specialist electrical training and then on to the Mediterranean Fleet and *HMS Liverpool*, a Town-class light cruiser with 6" guns. And it was while here that I saw a notice calling for volunteers for the Submarine Service.

I duly volunteered and, on return to UK, was posted to *HMS Dolphin* 2 for my training, after which I joined *HMS Alliance* – my first boat. Something I will never forget are the idiosyncrasies of life aboard a submarine where discipline, although strict, was dispensed with a relaxed informality. And where style of clothing was 'optional' to say the least, when the skipper sported a baseball cap and tee-shirt, and the chef wore a top hat. Further postings followed in quick succession until I joined my final boat – the 'A' Class *HMS Anchorite* based at Rothesay on the Isle of Bute. Our main task was to patrol the North Atlantic. Training was, I clearly remember, tough and uncompromising, where men and equipment were tested to the limits. I can remember one particular time on an exercise when an aircraft crashed into the cliffs of Northern Ireland with the loss of all on board, and another occasion when we ran aground on the mud. And then, on yet another unforgettable occasion we were straddled far too accurately by a pattern of live Hedgehogs (anti-submarine explosives), which made the boat drop like a stone for thirty feet or more with near fatal consequences.

On a lighter note I recall a moment akin to pure swashbuckling high seas chicanery. Due to a worldwide fuel crisis, we would meet up at night with a fishing trawler and exchange some of our diesel for crates of fresh cod, crab and lobster. Exactly how our shortage of fuel was explained away when we got back, neither I nor anyone else was allowed to know about. And again, on another occasion, when out in the Atlantic, after one of our main motors had failed, and after a futile and wholly unsatisfactory argument with Base, we were ordered to make for Chatham. A mighty storm then brewed and the boat, rolling heavily on the surface and with hatches open, began to take on water. At the mercy of the elements there was little we could do other than to be heartily sea sick, every man Jack of us. Life below was not always easy, you should understand.

I was demobbed in 1957, finishing my career as a Petty Officer (Electrician). Now a civvy, I lived first at Carshalton where I plied my trade as an electrician, initially for Ferranti and later for Rolls Royce in Derby. After a number of years a workmate persuaded me to leave the big firms and to come and work with him in South Molton, North Devon. I moved down in 1984 and not much later met Sheila to whom I became married in 1986. I first came into contact with the RBL through my own ill health a number of years ago, and am now firmly ensconced as a member of the South Molton Branch.

Looking back over my service life, I would do it all over again. Submariners are, I have to admit, a strange, piratical lot, yet a wonderful breed blessed with a unique 'esprit de corps.' In all my time at sea I cannot recall a single occasion when any member of the crew had to be charged formally and marched away. It was simply never necessary. Great people they were – undoubtedly the best years of my life.

Alex Ingleton
Army. Royal Wessex Yeomanry. Lance Corporal.

I was born in Margate, in 1983 – a man of Kent, so I am – from whence my father came also. My mother hailed from Hammersmith and grew up in London. Father was a train driver, still is, and we moved first to Whitstable and then, when I was about five, to the small village of Bishops Nympton, just outside South Molton. School days were fun – I was an average kid, in and out of scrapes with loads of friends, many of whom are close to me still. I was pretty average at sport but, from an early age, got interested in shooting. I got my first air rifle when eleven and the shot gun at fourteen. I really went for all types of shooting; both clays as well as game and vermin on friends' farms.

After leaving school I earned my first pennies as a farm labourer before going to the East Devon Tech to study Public Services. It was here that I first became interested in the military, encouraged by my grandfather who had done his National Service many years before. Then, after college, I worked for a local builder until temptation took me to sign on as a Regular. I just don't know why, but after only a few weeks of it I dropped out – a horrendous mistake. Happily though, I had friends in the local TA Squadron who encouraged me to join. I did, and I remain with them and have never looked back.

Selection was at Bovington followed closely by initial training at Wyvern Barracks, Exeter. Then came Basic Training which was tough, the graft aided and abetted by instructors from the Paras who booted us all over the place. Less than half of us survived the endless beasting and screaming, but I got there eventually and arrived in one piece at 'D' Squadron, The Royal Wessex Yeomanry – my military home. Irritatingly I just missed out on Iraq but there was always Afghanistan. Volunteers were called for and, as soon as I heard, I stepped forward. Training began in Jan 2010 when I learned that we were to be attached to 5 Regt RA in the locating role. In simplest terms, I was to be tasked to operate high powered cameras and radars. All 'High Tec' stuff, in fact £2.5m worth of kit on my signature, but it certainly paid its way.

Moving now to Afghanistan I, like everybody else, spent two weeks at Camp Bastion acclimatising and getting used to all our kit. I was then sent forward to FOB Jackson to join a company of 40 Commando, Royal Marines. Funnily enough I caught a glimpse (but didn't have a chance to chat to him) of Kevin Bateman, one of the Marines and another member of our South Molton Branch of the RBL. We had a number of successful contacts with this equipment. On one occasion a Marine had been wounded by a sniper and my cameras were able to pin point where the shot had come from. This was converted to an eight figure grid reference which we passed to the patrol who brought to bear a sixty mm anti-personnel rocket. Bingo! Great to watch on camera, especially to see bits of the bloke whirling high into the air.

Some time after this I was transferred to The Scots Guards. More fun here. On one operation we identified a group of seven Taliban setting up an ambush position some four kilometres away. We pinpointed their position and brought in an Apache strike with rockets and cannon. Another bulls eye – seven out of seven. Most popular of all was when we caught the Taleban setting up IEDs (the infantryman's horror) by the road side. We could see them clearly digging them in and would then introduce ourselves with a strike by Hellfire or with the Apaches. In amongst all my camera work came the inevitable patrolling. Fire fights came and went. I got away with it but when a round went through the water carrier on my back and soaked me, it felt like blood. I yelled that I'd been hit, only to have my dying shouts shut up by my mate, a Fijian, who was laughing his head off. That's close enough, thanks! The Guardsmen were a great bunch of lads with whom I made a number of really good chums and we still keep in touch. Astonishing really, seeing as I can't speak or write a word of Glaswegian. It was a tough time, though. Just before I arrived the position had lost a couple of lads and it was the middle of the Afghan summer – very, very hot with none of life's little luxuries to keep us cool.

Looking back I enjoyed the tour although there were horrible moments such as the time when we had to move in and clean up after an unfortunate US air strike on a group of civilians. The horrors of what we came across, in particular the children, is something we'll never forget. That said, I really do enjoy my soldiering and I'm getting in as much as I can. As I write this, I'm working my way towards my next tour out there, which may or may not come about before they call it a day. I joined the South Molton branch of the RBL in 2009 and I really enjoy it. There are lots of mates and we have a good time together.

Ken Jones
Army. Glosters. Corporal.

I was born on 14th March 1921 in Gloucester to Victor and Ilda Jones. My first memory of life is of a near neighbour who kept monkeys and the excitement one day when they escaped up his chimney. Early days were not particularly happy as I was only four when my parents divorced and I went to live with my father in Banbury, who was a WWI veteran with the Cheshire Regt. He was employed on the railways, where he finished up as manager. Not unnaturally I followed him; my first job aged fourteen being as a 'greaser'. For something less than £1 per week my task was to keep the axle boxes filled with grease. Later I was promoted to work in the engine sheds as an engine cleaner. All that shiny metal, gleaming brass and the smell of steam – a dream for most youngsters!

When I was seventeen I joined the Ox and Bucks TA. Later that year, I became a Regular with The Glosters at Horfield Barracks, Bristol. The first month was sheer agony – my muscles simply did not belong to me. However, matters improved. Eventually it was fantastic: I was marvellously fit, helped along by the tough infantry training. Although pay was just seven shillings a week, life was very full. Once a week each of us in the room put a shilling on the table and one of us had an evening out, but in uniform. My mother bought me a set of Regimental Blues which helped things along, but nothing really exciting – perhaps the cinema followed by fish 'n chips before catching the tram back to barracks.

Then, come Spring 1939, I was posted to the Glosters 2nd Battalion who were in Seaton Barracks, Plymouth. I was trained as a drummer/bugler and it was there that I first caught sight of the 'new' Bren gun and the Boys anti-tank rifle. When war broke out I was still not yet eighteen so was posted to Liverpool where we were attached to the Royal Engineers checking ammunition and other equipment which had arrived from America. Later we were moved along the canal to Manchester to do the same job. Then came the blitz. We were billeted in Transport House at Old Trafford and I well remember the night we suffered a direct hit and were bombed out. The reason we escaped with our lives was because we were sheltering down in the cellars. I then caught severe pneumonia, so badly that when I came round I saw my father sitting on the bed. He had been sent for in case the worst should happen! I went back to the Glosters but was medically downgraded and posted to the Military Police as a VP (Vulnerable Post), destined for special guard duties.

Exciting at times, we were constantly on the move as it was decided that we should never stay in the same place for long because we would learn too much. I remember duties at Bletchley Park, at the Top Secret Government base at Blenheim, at the huge ammo Depot near Bath and various secret radar installations here and there. It was when serving in Cornwall that I met Jenny, my wife, who was serving in the ATS attached to the Royal Artillery.

Not long afterwards I found myself at Stokes Bay in Gosport where we boarded an LST (Tank Landing Craft). Our task was to follow immediately behind the D-Day assault troops and take control of prisoners. We landed on D+1, running ashore as soon as the ramp had crashed down into the shallow water. We could distinctly hear the sound of gunfire not far ahead of us and I remember a lot of debris on the beach – burned out vehicles, destroyed equipment and numerous bodies that had yet to be collected. The prisoners were waiting for us under guard and we escorted them back to the LST, and made our way back to Southampton. Here the prisoners were met by an armed guard and herded into cages before undergoing interrogation. On one occasion we took charge of a German Military Hospital that had been captured at Brussels. This time we did not hand them over at Southampton, rather we took them by train to a camp just south of Inverness. Here the suspected Nazi sympathisers were separated from the remainder who were returned to the south coast, where they were to set up a military hospital to cater for the wounded German POWs.

Somehow, amid all this turmoil, Jenny and I were married. My war ended in London where, after a short interview, I emerged as a civvy with my demob suit. I remained in the Reserves for a further six years. Work, post-war, was not easy to find but I went to Thorneycrofts in Southampton, proved to the interviewers that I had learned a skill as a French polisher and was taken on – working at this and other trades until my eventual retirement. I should add that I joined the ACF as an adult instructor and that all my boys followed me into the ACF, several of them moving on into man service in the Army.

It was Jenny who decided that we should settle in the West Country. During the war she had served near Bude when serving with the Royal Artillery. She loved it down here so, in 1989, we moved to South Molton. I had joined the RBL years before at Banbury in the early sixties. The South Molton Branch was, at that time in suspended animation but was later rejuvenated, and I was able to join them. I enjoy my time with the Legion – it's the comradeship which, in a good Branch, is the next best thing to that which one finds in the Regulars.

John Keene
Royal Air Force. MTD. Senior Aircraftman.

I was born at 104 Escott Hill in the railway town of Swindon, Wilts, in 1938. I was the fourth child of nine and I look back on my childhood days as being a wonderful time, when I and my siblings had nothing but each other and our friends for company. My one and only really sad memory was when a chum who lived nearby was run over and killed. But that's all part of life, I have to admit, but something one never forgets. School I tolerated, but it was here that I found the Air cadets – together with dreams of becoming a fighter pilot.

Leaving school at fifteen, life took me first to work in a laundry and from there to a fishmonger where I learned to drive – happily doing the rounds for my boss. Call up papers arrived when I was seventeen and a half: not unexpectedly as my older brothers had received theirs previously; one of them, Jim, seeing active service with the Glosters in Korea. I duly packed my one small bag, and reported to RAF Cardington. Here, while waiting to be interviewed, I saw the station ambulance going past so, as I already had my driving licence, decided that a career driving something less exotic might be a safer bet.

Next came RAF Wilmslow for the dreaded Basic Training. It was pure hell and even now I can remember the face of the horrendous Drill Corporal who reduced men to tears and who we all roundly detested until, having passed off the square, we all met up for drinks and became firm friends. HGV driver training was at Weeton Camp near Blackpool, and here I met up with some chums from bygone Swindon days whose company made me feel that life was not so bad after all. Late 1956 saw me posted to RAF Hullavington where I joined the MT Section. Station life was pretty cushy, due in the main to the fact that I was a pretty fair footballer and was picked to play inside left not only for our Station but for Bomber Command. The CO was dead keen to win; so much so that he took the footballers and other sportsmen off dress parades, fatigues and other unpleasant camp duties.

That said, life was, by today's standards, basic indeed. Living twenty to a room, I came across those who hailed from far beyond Swindon. Nicknamed 'Farmer' on account of my rich Westcountry accent, I watched in amazement as Geordies, Jocks, London Cockneys, Scousers and the Welsh tried to understand one another. Even so there were more friends from home whose faces I remembered. Naturally enough there was the barrack room bully, but he was hunted down, thrown into a cold bath and held under until he had stopped wriggling. No more nonsense from him, that was for sure!

Perhaps my most abiding memory of all was the fact that Hullavington was the end of the road for many of the bombers from WWII. Giant Lincolns and Lancasters would fly slowly in to await the scrap merchants' hammers and blowtorches. The aircraft, once they had landed and taxied away, were parked up on the outer fringes of the airfield. By this time I had been trained as a crane driver and it was my task to lift the huge Merlin engines out of the airframes. On some days, when fresh aircraft came in, I would get sandwiches from the cookhouse and go out alone to visit these old warriors as they stood silent and still, as though waiting patiently for their next mission. With nobody around, I would climb aboard and sit where the aircrew used to sit all those years ago, as the aircraft ground their way across Europe for King and Country. Although every boys' dream it was, nevertheless, poignant to see the end of these grand old veterans that had served us so faithfully.

And it was here, at Hullavington, that I met my wife, Jo, who was serving alongside me, as a member of the WAAF. Love at first sight so it was, our courtship began in the heady and romantic environment of the Station NAAFI. We were married in Swindon soon afterwards but, being denied the luxury of a married quarter, life together began in a caravan perched on the periphery of the base; a situation that saw the pair of us either cycling or walking to work each morning. Demob came in November 1959 when I took the short journey back home to Swindon. Having put our names down for a council house, I began work for a haulage firm, later following the money first as a scaffolder and then into the building trade.

We first came across North Devon while on a touring holiday and it was when I was forced to take early retirement as a result of heart problems that we decided to move westwards, settling eventually in South Molton. Here I found myself among several already in the Legion, so I decided to join. It was a good way to make new friends, both that and for that wonderful ex-Service camaraderie you can't find anywhere else.

Charlie Kingdom
Reserved Occupation. Farmer.

Author's Note.
This is Charlie Kingdom's story of service during the last war in the Reserved Occupation Scheme. This was initiated in 1938 and at its height involved five million men that included farmers, doctors, miners, and railway and dock workers.   This explanation has been included with this story as it was felt that those employed within this scheme rarely received the recognition that they rightly deserved. Its inclusion here is in keeping with the aim of this book, to provide a wide range of stories portraying activities over the years of all those who served their Country. Not all were called to arms and many of those who were not, worked the land and played an integral part in maintaining and supporting the war effort on the Home Front. They were destined to play a vital role after some found themselves in a somewhat less than glamorous occupation, during the period of the conflict. Charlie's story includes a farming calendar which provides an insight into a typical farm workers year of the period. This is his story in his own words.

I was born 3 June 1927 at Broxbridge Cottage, Exebridge, Dulverton. My family was Mother and Father with Robert, my half brother, William Henry Kingdom and Albert Edward Kingdom, All three brothers joined the Home Guard when old enough. I went to three schools, Molland, Bishops Nympton and Wheddon Cross. I left school when I was 14 on 14 August 1941, and went to work at Middle Ball, Twitchen, farming. When not working on the farm I used to like to go to the cinema and I enjoyed the local whist drives.

Later when I was old enough to be called up I didn't go into the military but was told I was to stay farming and work in the Reserved Occupation as they called it. I had no choice, but I wasn't bothered and so I just carried on with the farming. My Mother and Father were pleased and so was I. Some might think that I should have wanted to go but I was working hard and 'doing my bit' as they used to say. It was hard work and plenty to do, early mornings, late into the night sometimes, and any time that you were needed and in all weathers. I enjoyed my work.

A Farming Year at Middleball Farm

18 August 1941 I went on a farm called Middleball farm, Twitchen, to help with the sheep. Cattle October time, young cattle went indoors for the winter. October was pulling mangols (sic), put into caves. November was pulling swedes. Every day the cattle was fed Swedes, hay also turnips. Swedes for sheep. Cows came in, in December, for the winter. They were fed hay and corn. I fed the sheep with a horse cart. March 14th was lambing time out doors which had to be seen every hour. At the end of April cattle would go out to grass. At the end of May I helped dock sheep. Grass was cut at the end of June. I helped shear sheep. Mangols (sic) were tilled at the end of May, swedes were tilled at the beginning of June. Corn tilled in April. At the end of June hay was made. Corn was cut middle of August. In 1943 we had a Fordson tractor on spade logs with iron wheels. Yellow tractor was on wheels. In 1955 we had a new David Brown tractor and a new baler which baled the hay. In 1957 he bought a Ferguson Tractor, 35 horsepower. I left the farm in June 1960.

Life was very different in those days. None of the luxuries like you have today; no central heating, coal and wood for the hot water, tin baths and out down the garden for the Privy, bad luck if it was snow. Clothes were boiled in the copper and wash boards to scrub them. You thought nothing of it, you just got on. There was food rationing too. People today would not like that. Limited food and sweets and sugar stuff for the children. You had a special book with all coupons in it. Buy something and get the coupons cut out. You had to be careful with everything, even the clothes. 'Make do and mend' they called it.

I joined the Legion in South Molton in 1991. I enjoy the company and feel at home when I have a good chat with some of the old boys like me and the young ones too. It is really a nice feeling and we are supporting a charity that does real good for the military.

Ian Kingdon
Army. Royal Tank Regiment. Lance Corporal.

I'm a farmer's boy having been born in South Molton Cottage Hospital in 1967 as the youngest of four. We grew up on our farm at West Buckland where I remember stories of my uncle who had served in the Devons. A while later we moved to Brayford, and I was sent to West Buckland School. No academic, I lived for my sport and was there with Jonathan Edwards, the triple jump Gold Medallist, and Victor Obogu the England rugby player with whom I played on the school XV. While at school I also joined the CCF and for three years we did the Ten Tors march on Dartmoor.

I left at sixteen, worked on the farm for a bit and then joined the Army. My initial choice was for the Sappers (Royal engineers) but I failed the aptitude tests and so opted for the Royal Tank Regiment. Basic Training was up at Catterick in Yorkshire and was the usual catalogue of horrors. Almost half our intake of fifty-five dropped out, the twelve mile marches that included the water tunnel catching most of them. I always remember the charming instructor who inspected our kit. 'Chose a window', he would ask disarmingly. Once the victim had made his selection, out would go all his kit, every single item and we were way up on the second floor. Looking back I suppose it was pretty much as expected in those days, and I was luckier than most in that I was asked to turn out for the Training Regiment's rugby team. Eventually the posting order came through and I, together with two others, was off to Paderborn in Germany, my new home being 3 RTR.

Life for the new boy in 1985 was really pretty quiet, in fact I was almost totally ignored for some time – an initiation endured by all newcomers. While at Catterick I had done my driver training and found my new job as a driver. Here, though, there was snow and a Chieftan tank on snow is like a sixty-ton duck on ice. Unsteady! Once again rugby broke the routine for me and any weekend we were not training there was a game somewhere or other. Training was hard and realistic – we were only fifty miles from our war deployment positions. My most abiding memories were of the constant maintenance and repairs our beasts required. Many a night spent under the stars groping around with the engine decks open. That and the cold: on one occasion it was down to minus twenty and, when you're static in the open, that's cold. It was here that I was awarded the C-in-C's commendation for my assistance at a severe accident.

When training up north at Bergen Hohne we went and visited the Belsen concentration camp. Now a museum, it was a grim and sobering experience, almost unbelievable what man could do to fellow man. On a more cheerful note there were the visits to the delights of Hamburg where we young tearaways would set the Reeperbahn alight – drawn in by the bright lights that got redder and redder. While here we were sent to Canada for six weeks live firing at Batus, the big training area, at the end of which we went down to Calgary to see how the cowboys lived in cowboy country. A bit later we sent a composite squadron to Cyprus. I was ordered to go (one of the best orders I've had!). We were part of the UK Sovereign Base contingent and drove Saladin Armoured cars and Ferret Scout Cars. Great fun but there were a number of terrorist incidents including the families being mortared on the beach and one of our drivers being shot and wounded.

Back to Germany and we were posted to Iserlohn near Dortmund where we changed our Chieftans for the newer Challengers. Much the same routine, it was endless training and the annual trip to Canada for live firing. I got promoted to L/Cpl and then upwards to Acting Sergeant for the Nuclear, Biological and Chemical Warfare training. It was after our Canada trip that we first felt the hand of the IRA when a Sergeant was murdered and, when I was Guard Commander, a party was surprised breaking in to our camp. Soon afterwards we were warned off for Op Banner (Northern Ireland). I was deployed to the border town of Middletown. The reception committee did not wait long and within a couple of hours we had our first car bomb. A week later three RUC officers and a civilian were killed nearby. Amazingly we arrived in the middle of a heatwave and for six weeks roasted in our flak jackets – but then came the rain, and how. Everything had to be done on foot or by heli. Our main problem was with the constant cross-border sniping and car bombs that killed several policemen. Intelligence told us that our camp was a prime target but, thankfully, the opposition decided otherwise.

By this time I had had enough and by the time we got back to Germany my cards were in. Promised six weeks leave for our efforts, the Regiment was 'stood to' after a just week, for Iraq, but were not deployed due to the very short duration of the war, and I came home. After a number of driving jobs and a good long holiday travelling the world I decided to become a driving instructor. I now have my own business and am well settled here with wife and family, the youngest of whom is eight. In 2009 I joined the South Molton Branch of the RBL. I enjoy it and recent events in Afghanistan have shown us all just what an important charity the organisation is.

Paddy King-Fretts
Army. The Devonshire and Dorset Regiment. Colonel.

Born in 1941, I grew up on a small, remote hill farm high in the wilds of Exmoor. Back then, life was mighty tough up there but a great preparation for what lay ahead. Educated at Sherborne, I found my way to Sandhurst in 1959. After commissioning I joined my regiment in Plymouth where I was given command of a platoon of National Servicemen. They had been ordered to do an extra six months but with no additional pay (then £1.50 per week). They were not impressed, either with their misfortune or their new platoon commander – with nothing, in fact.

First whiff of active service came when we were sent to British Guyana. Here the Afro-Caribbean and Indian communities were at each others throats and we were ordered to get between them and sort things out. We did, only to find that both sides often decided to have a go at us. Sometimes it all went mad, like the time when a riot, in full swing, was joined by a festive steel band complete with calypso dancers. Soon after returning home I volunteered for and passed into 22 SAS. Back then the Regiment was operating in Aden and my troop was engaged in operations in Aden town and the Crater district. A few months later we were sent up to the Radfan where we saw the last of the mountain operations. The Radfani tribesman were utterly ruthless and excellent shots. Mistakes were punished mercilessly.

Back with my old battalion, I found myself on something of a dream holiday posting to Malta – but not for long. The Ulster emergency was raging and we were hurriedly deployed to Belfast. Even now, memories of shots being fired in a British capital city, of rows of houses burning, and of soldiers, police and civilians being killed seems astonishing. A second tour to a rural area was followed by Staff College and then it was back to the SAS to command 'A' Squadron. The Dhofar war was at its height, and the fighting on the jebel was hard going. We took a number of casualties yet returned home with a healthy scorecard. A second tour followed at the end of which came a shock. I was off to Germany! Life out there was nothing more than a series of vast war games played out, by us on one side and by the Russians on the other.

Rome came next: preparation for a posting to a NATO appointment in Holland where I was the Personal Assistant to General von Senger und Etterlin, the C-in-C of NATO's Central Region. The General, a marvelous man and a great Anglophile, had lost his right arm at the battle of Stalino when it was amputated under local anaesthetic on the engine deck of a tank, whose engine was kept running so that he would not freeze to death. While here I witnessed NATO rehearsing full nuclear war when, deep underground inside the command bunker, the red buttons were pressed to order General Nuclear Release – quite unforgettable, unreal.

Command of my own Regiment followed in 1982 and it was not long before we were back in Ulster, this time for two years. Sent to live in a quiet backwater well out of harm's way, but with my soldiers operating with other regiments, life could easily have become unimaginably dull. To keep myself sane I went off and joined my soldiers. Somewhat unconventionally, I used to take off all badges of rank and join them as a simple rifleman on their patrols. Ballymurphy and Crossmaglen were, without doubt, the hot spots where, time and again, patrols were either shot up or blown up. If I was asking them to do this day after day then I needed to get out there and do it with them. Hairy, yes, but wonderful, exhilarating stuff being back on the front line. And it was here that my admiration for the British soldier reached such heights. To go out on patrol day after day, for weeks on end knowing well that sooner or later you were going to have a contact, requires steadiness and courage of the very highest order. These tremendous qualities, shown again today by our young soldiers in Afghanistan, can only be wondered at. To fully understand this you have to get out there and actually do it. Every politician should be made to do just that, once – as a 'squaddie', in full kit, with weapons, radio and in the heat of the day. That would get them thinking!

My last few years were spent in England, first in Aldershot and then at The School of Infantry. After Army life, it was a complete change when we moved to France to run a small holiday business for ten years before coming home to roots. Looking back there are so many fond memories. Sometimes it was tough but more often it was a great life, living and working with wonderful people. A number of men, some very good friends, were lost but my own luck held, and I managed to survive with barely a scratch. On active service one has to be philosophical. It's no good worrying about what might happen; you've just got to get on with it.

So, why the Legion? It's time to put something back into the kitty. The RBL caters for everyone in the Services who has fallen on hard times. It's very rewarding being able to help. Here in South Molton we have built up a tremendous branch into something of which we can be justly proud. They're a great bunch of people and I believe that, together, we really do our bit for the great cause. Long may it continue.

Terence Lavercombe
Army. Royal Electrical and Mechanical Engineers. Craftsman.

Born in 1933 at Bishops Tawton, I came into this world as the eldest of three, and into a military family, my father having served throughout the war in the Royal Army Ordnance Corps. I was educated at Barnstaple Boys Grammar School where I lived for my sports – cricket in the Summer and rugby throughout the Winter. After school I undertook five years training as a mechanical engineering draughtsman. During this time I played rugby for South Molton, the pitch being on a windy hillside out in the wilds and our changing room at the back of a now-defunct pub.

The long awaited call up papers arrived in June 1955 when I was invited to present myself at Blandford Forum station where luxury 3-ton Bedford Military transport took me to Anson and Craddock Barracks for induction and trade testing for the Royal Electrical and Mechanical Engineers (REME). After about ten days of medicals, jabs, trade tests, parades and boot polishing we proceeded to Barton Stacey camp near Winchester to commence our basic training. The man in charge of us was a Company Sergeant Major of the South Wales Borderers who had lost his right arm on D-Day. This did not prevent him doing an excellent job – his salutes with the left arm being a speciality. Life here was pretty basic. We were billeted twenty to a wooden hut with a coke fire in the middle of the room. Bedding was a straw palliase. Reveille was at some ungodly hour when the NCOs would come crashing into the room, shouting and screaming and hauling out of bed those who had not jumped to it immediately. And here we lived and slept, pressing our kit on the one table and drying anything that got wet around the fire. The stench of flesh, sweat and wet clothes remains to this day!

After passing out I was posted to 5 Battalion REME at Arborfield, near Reading for a six month course on the intricacies of the No 11 Anti-aircraft predictor, and the 3.7" anti-aircraft gun. By this time conventional AA warfare was on the wane and ours was the last course. Just three weeks before our arrival the IRA had raided the armoury and stolen a number of weapons. The size of the guard that greeted us had to be seen to be believed. No weapons though: intruders would have been brought to their knees by pick helves. The difference here was that the NCOs were of two types – Regimental and Technical. At one point I was ordered to get my haircut by the RSM (Regimental). After the parade I was collared by the S/Sgt (Technical) who told me to take no notice of the silly old so and so. 'He just says the man fourth along in the middle rank – get a haircut, the eighth man in the rear rank – dirty boots. Just keep moving yourself around each time'.

After completing trade training I was posted to 6 Armoured Workshops REME in Osnabruck, North Germany where, surprise, surprise, there was no Ack Ack, only tanks. A quick conversion course at Duisburg brought me up to scratch on that wonderful tank, the Centurion, specifically the gun control equipment and stabilizers. The Centurion was way ahead of its time, having proved itself in Korea and with its gun stabilizing ability. We divided our time between, in the Summer the delights of Luneburg Heath and the fleshpots of Hamburg. The Reeperbahn and St Pauli Districts of Hamburg, the reader should understand, are where young men a long way from home grew up very quickly indeed.

In Winter months my memory takes me back to the freezing WWII German Army Barracks in which we lived – thank goodness for the British NAAFI, with its warmth, its cups of hot sweet tea and its cigarettes that cost us one shilling and three pence (7p today) for packs of forty. We worked hard though. As our workshop was surrounded by armoured regiments, we always had plenty to do.

Demob came for me in June 1957 when I transferred to the Army Emergency Reserve to continue my reserve commitment, rather than the Territorials. I had thought of converting to a regular commitment but my wife-to-be had very firm but very different ideas. Christine and I were married in 1959 and now have a fine family, including six grandchildren. My life now evolved around various jobs in the manufacturing and mechanical engineering industries until retirement caught up with me in 1993.

A few years earlier we had moved from Barnstaple to South Molton. I had not had much contact with the Legion during this time but in 2011, Bill Webber, the previous Branch Chairman and a good friend, persuaded me that perhaps membership would be a good idea. Indeed I have found it so with the comradeship and inspiration.

Peter Leach
*Army. Royal Hussars/ Kings Royal Hussars,
Royal Wessex Yeomanry. Staff Sergeant.*

Born in 1959, I joined the Royal Green Jackets cadets in 1972, beginning in Winchester. First morning, and with lots of shouting, I saw recruits sweeping the square with tooth brushes. Not for me, I thought! I was, in fact, bound initially for the Navy but was accosted by a smart, but fierce-looking S/Sgt in his crimson trousers. 'Not the Navy, lad,' he advised me. 'They have to swim a lot'. The Navy recruiters were way up on the top floor, the RAF on the next, and the cunning Army down on the ground floor where potential recruits, like me, could be ambushed. I was, and duly signed on for the Royal Armoured Corps Junior Leaders in April 1976. A year later, I passed out as a Chieftan gunner/radio operator and joined 'C' Squadron of the Royal Hussars who went to Denmark. All hell kicked off when the Danes were found to be using a Union flag to clean their weapons. We weighed in. Heavily outnumbered, we held our own until the Danish MPs separated us. Misunderstandings were resolved, added to which, the Danes paid for the beer.

On returning to Germany we found Northern Ireland (Op Banner) looming, our mission being to control the Belfast City Centre. My own task was to be a 'spotter' as I could recognise faces at a glance, and also as a searcher in a 'sniffer' team. Eventually I found myself with 41 Commando in the notorious Lower Falls area. Working with the Marines and their strange ways entailed a steep learning curve. My first patrol was one that was tasked to visit pubs and clubs. On entering 'The Pound Club' all the lights went out. The Marines IA was to fire two baton rounds at the ceiling of what was effectively a concrete bunker, the two projectiles immediately becoming unguided missiles ricocheting around. At once the lights came back on – everyone trying to avoid the high speed projectiles. The two suspects we were looking for were found outside, dazed and bruised but little worse for wear.

Back to Germany we were threatened to return to Catterick as the Training Regiment. Definitely not my cup of tea, I volunteered for Belize. I trained as a 30mm Rarden cannon gunner and, in Jan 1979, found myself at Holdfast camp. I did my jungle training, trained in survival by the SAS team there. Canoeing also. Albeit it inside the barrier reef, nevertheless capsize drills took place under the gaze of barracuda, Hammerhead and Tiger sharks. A healthy encouragement to get back in sharpish, to say the least! On returning to Catterick I was due to be posted on a Drill Instructors course. Again, not my idea of fun, I remonstrated and found myself in Smuts Barracks, Berlin which overlooked Spandau Prison where Rudolph Hess was incarcerated. We would see him pottering about in his garden when the Brits or Americans were guarding him, but come the Russians and he would remain under lock and key.

After two years of being split up to the four winds, the Regiment regrouped at Fallingbostel. This was to be an eight year posting, when we were the first to convert to the Challenger tank. We got back to the UK just in time to miss being the lead battle group for the Gulf War. I went off to Belize again, ten years on, only to find the same wrecked car in the same place outside the main gate. Another dose of jungle training where we met all our old creepy crawly friends – at one point a giant tarantula kept the lads standing on their beds. Soon after returning to Germany I learned that my troop had been selected for Iraq where we deployed in Jan 1990. The build up was outstanding and the vehicles were prepared as well as could be. We moved up to Hafir Al Batin just in time to be in the target area for Scud missiles. After this welcome we moved out in to the desert and dug in. Screams and yells one morning as my driver dashed hither and thither. His shorts were in shreds and his crown jewels scratched and bleeding. A family of jerboas had taken over his sleeping bag as their home, and had put up a spirited resistance when the rightful owner climbed in with them.

After crossing into Iraq, we got a number of sharp wake-up calls. The first was witnessing the devastating effect of our main tank armament (Armour piercing 120 mm) had on the substandard Soviet and Chinese armoured vehicles. We came across only anti-personnel mines but my tank claimed two Chinese T-59 main battle tanks. Next, and equally sobering, was the effect that American aircraft fire had on our Warrior vehicles. After the 'Blue on Blue' we were instructed to find orange day-glow panels or 'something like it' with which to mark the top of our vehicles. All we could manage was the vest of our despatch rider, which we borrowed (he didn't really need it anyway). Then came the appalling sight of the carnage along the Basra highway and, finally, the oil field fires that turned night into day.

I finished Regular service and for the next three years was the Admin S/NCO with 'B' Sqn, Royal Wessex Yeomanry. When the chance came to move to 'D' Squadron, I took it immediately and moved in 2003. My one sad moment was in 2009 when I was appointed Visiting Officer to the mother of a young soldier killed in Afghanistan. We did all that we could to help and I'm proud to say that, for this, I was awarded the GOC's commendation. I am still serving with 'D' Squadron and recently joined the South Molton Branch of the RBL

John 'Spud' Leaning
Army. Royal Artillery. Major.

I was born in Highgate, London on the 15th May 1937. Eighteen years later, I entered the Royal Military Academy, Sandhurst and passed out in 1957, commissioned into the Royal Artillery. My first command was a troop of four 5.5 inch guns in Edinburgh with 21 Medium Regiment. After two years there I was posted to the British Army of the Rhine (BAOR), Germany, at Munster where 40 Field Regt had 25 pounders. Here we seemed to be permanently on exercise, live firing or playing sport. Sport became my preoccupation. The Regiment were Army Ski Champions for five successive years: I was determined to make the team, and eventually got there. Then, something of a shock when I was sent to Troon to instruct at the Junior Tradesmen's Regiment. Initially I ran Z Stream, commander (or nursemaid) to twenty-six of the little blighters.

Escape at last in 1965 when I was picked up for the National Biathlon Team, when we went to Norway to train for the 1968 Winter Olympics. I was appointed team captain, manager and reserve athlete. However I was also studying for the Staff College and was a Troop Commander in 94 Locating Regiment. Talk about 'all go' and divided aims! Anyhow, with 94 Regiment we won the Army Ski championship three times and went on to an Olympic Winter Games (OWG). What's more I managed to pass the Staff College exam. Before going to Camberley, which I found pretty hard going, I was sent to Gibraltar with my Robert Radar Troop. Spain was making threatening noises and we were wanted to survey the approaches to the Rock from the mainland.

After Staff College, I was sent to Northumbrian District at Catterick as a staff officer. Stultifyingly boring, the only excitements were strikes and support to the civil community. Eventually I escaped and, in 1972, aged thirty-five, I passed the Commando Course and joined 45 Commando Group in Arbroath. Here I was in command of 145 (Maiwand) Commando Light Battery of 105mm pack howitzers and over-snow vehicles. Our task was the protection of NATO's Northern Flank, north of Norway. We spent much time Arctic training. Hard going it was from January to the end of March, with Arctic survival and major exercises where we lived in ten man tents when the temperature fell to minus forty degrees.

In July 1974 we went to Northern Ireland. 45 Commando, with nine hundred men, was larger than a battalion as they had the extra subunit of our 145 Battery. 45 Commando was on the border at Newry and we went to Armagh to come under command of the Lifeguards. What a contrast between the Green Berets and the Lifeguards! However we were given our own area to control, based mainly at Coagh and Dungannon and left to our own devices. We had an active time, meeting hostile activity and aggression from the opposition more than adequately with our own. Time flew, we took no casualties and came away knowing we had done an effective job: it was a privilege to command such outstanding soldiers. Experience gained with the Navy and Royal Marines had been interesting and informative. Following this came another staff job with 1 Division in Verden, Germany. Combining artillery logistics with general administrative support for Verden Garrison was hard work indeed - an enormous workload.

Larkhill followed, where I was Executive Officer to the Force Artillery of the Allied Mobile Force (Land), embracing UK, German, Belgium, Canadian, Italian and US gun batteries. Our role was that we had to be prepared to deploy at any time to either of the NATO flanks, and it fell to me to plan, write and oversee the main exercises. After this I was sent to Bulford, responsible for staff planning for the whole of the UK Mobile contingent – basically a complete Battle Group. Winter training took place in Norway and I saw, immediately, that the UK Contingent Arctic training was inadequate, way below that of the Royal Marines. Based on their doctrine, I rewrote the training manuals and borrowed, from HQ Commando Forces, fourteen Mountain Leader Instructors to train the contingent. Needless to say, standards improved markedly.

Then came the RAF, when I was posted to RAF Odiham in Hampshire as Ground Liaison Officer to 7 Squadron (Chinooks). Something of a challenge here as I had to change the mindset of the squadron as to how they were perceived by the Army and the tasks the Army expected of them. I left the Army in 1987 and worked for the British Ski Federation as the Director of Nordic Disciplines. I had had Olympic experience at two Winter Games already and, while here, took in a further three. Finally, I touched base with the Army once more when I worked at the Army Sport Control Board running Boxing and Swimming. Following this I lectured at Reading University on 'Leadership in Sport' for two Autumns.

So, why South Molton and the RBL? My wife died in 2002 leaving me with a sixteen year-old and a twenty-two year-old. My wife was brought up in Woolacombe and we had planned to move down to North Devon on retirement. I waited until my younger child had completed university and then decamped to South Molton, which I had got to know over the years when visiting family and for holidays. It is a decision I have never regretted and it has been an honour to be a member of the thriving British Legion community.

*****

Mike Livett
Army. Royal Electrical and Mechanical Engineers. Lance Corporal.

I was born in the beautiful Kentish countryside in 1948. At the time my father was a junior police officer with the Metropolitan Police. During the war years, however, he served with the RAF as a navigator/wireless operator when he met my mother 'over the airwaves' as she was a WAAF plotter. Both my uncles were in the RAF, one ending up as a Master Technican, and the eldest as a Group Captain in Whitehall. So, it would appear that the life cycle was to carry on with, eventually, myself joining one or other of the services.

Like most who joined post-war, any thoughts of an easy life were quickly dashed by bellowing Sergeant Majors during those first few hectic weeks. However, I would put myself through it all again; it was an experience that none of us would have missed. Eventually the training period was over and it was time to be sent out into the real world. My first posting to Cyprus was an eye-opener! First time away from Blighty and what better way to start, in a beautiful country and working with a multi-national force. I spent a spell on recovery duty within the workshops, giving me the opportunity to see both something of the countryside and to enjoy the job. Never a dull moment.

I remember one particular day when a number of us had travelled from Nicosia to Dhekelia in a 3 tonner, for a 'do' at the base workshops. Drink was taken and some four hours later we were on our way back. Unfortunately for us a Canadian Military

Police crew decided that our truck looked suspicious, and the drunken singing raised eyebrows even higher. Anyway they decided to pull us over and look further. Then came the questions. Unfortunately for us, one bright spark in the back (and you always get one when stopped by the 'Snowballs') decided it was time for some backchat. Any of you who have had any experience with the Military Police will understand that this is not wise. "We're on our way back from a vicar's tea party," blurted the loud voice. "What the f… does it look like?" Well, after three and a half hours in the Police cells at Nicosia and much fast talking, we were allowed on our way. Sober, yes, but still laughing uproariously. But that's life in the forces…go with it and enjoy every moment for what it's worth.

During my time in the UN workshops, a couple of colleagues encouraged me to apply for a posting to their unit when my time in Cyprus was up. Following a successful application in June 1967, I was on my way to Devon. As part of this elite unit, 18 Amphibious Squadron RCT, I found that we were on 24/7 call to anywhere in the country where our amphibious vehicles could be used. All drivers and mechanics were required to be masters in both radio and semaphore for communication, and fully trained seamen when we were on sea or river.

One particular situation I was involved with was an exercise on the Isle of Skye, working with a TA Royal Engineer unit from Liverpool, who had been tasked with erecting a number of ropewalks across lochs on the island. These walks were to assist access by the Search and Rescue teams when dealing with those lost or injured. I was responsible for the maintenance and full availability of the three DUKWs during the exercise, especially as they had to carry explosives, ropes, 1.5-ton stanchions plus the engineers themselves. The beauty of using this type of vehicle was that we could load all the equipment from the beach straight on to the 'Ducks' and then drive into the sea and on to the required destination.

A little about the DUKW: The vehicle originated from a standard GMC 6-wheeled US truck. In 1943 it was decided that an amphibious craft was required for various operations. The wheeled truck version was stripped of bodywork and re-fitted with a watertight hull, various other pieces plus the ingenious ability to increase or decrease air pressure to a single or combination of tyres while driving along. This enabled the driver to navigate across every type of sandy and muddy condition, 'Reading the Road' and changing pressures to suit the terrain.

Each of the DUKWs had a capability of carrying a 1.5-ton payload, which could either consist of a single vehicle, stores or twenty-two fully equipped troops. Many of you will recall how these vehicles covered themselves with glory on numerous occasions during WWII, nowhere more so than during the D-day landings. These same vehicles are still running today, albeit as civilian craft and can be found on the River Thames taking sightseers on trips up and down the river. Now in the evening of their lives, these marvellous old warhorses have really earned their place in history.

Back to my story.

Following the closure of the Amphibious unit in 1970, most vehicles went for scrap, but a few made it to Marchwood, Southampton for a number of years. Eventually these went, too, and the military DUKW is sadly no more. With the closure of 18 Amphibious Squadron RCT, I was then posted to Bulford, where I saw out my last days in the forces, leaving finally in June 1972.

I returned back to Devon to my new wife and young family where I continued to work as an engineer for the next thirty years with a company supplying equipment to the MOD. In 2007 I made two significant changes to my lifestyle. The first was to change my job and the second was to become a member of the South Molton Branch of the RBL.

And at the end of all this what can one say but 'Happy Days!'

*****

Katie Lovett
Army. Royal Army Medical Corps. Corporal.

I was born in Reading, Berkshire in 1971 to Terry and Angela. My father worked in the city itself as a shopping centre manager. We lived here until I was eight when we went to Milton Keynes – following Dad's work. My first memories of life were of the infant school at Eversley. I remember my time in the Brownies and I loved it there – didn't want to leave at all. Happily we were only at Milton Keynes for a year or so, and then moved down to the Exmoor town of Dulverton in West Somerset. I was very happy there, making lots of friends and enjoying the Youth Club. After finishing my schooling, I went on to college at Taunton to study Family and Community care. Even at this stage I found myself being drawn towards the world of medical care.

I enjoyed my time in Taunton but my parents moved to Sherborne in Dorset, this time to run a pub. I didn't want to go, preferring to stay in the Dulverton and Taunton area. But I eventually moved up with them and found work for two years in an old folks' home in Sherborne. After that I became a living-in nanny to a farming family in Cranborne, but not for long. I applied for and was accepted as House Matron at St Anthony's, a girls' school in Sherborne, again drawn by the world of care and welfare, in particular towards working with children.

Then came a break. I left and decided to take a job for six months working as a Children's Representative with Thompson's Holidays in Malta. It was a lot harder than I thought – forty screaming kids aged between four and eleven, without their parents and all on a great holiday can be problematical, and I found myself taxed to the very limit! At this point, initial thoughts of a military career began to emerge, first as a Dental Nurse with the RAF. But there was a waiting list so, on returning from Malta, I tried my hand at a number of things but nothing really appealed. One of the jobs, however, took me to Westward Ho! in North Devon. And it was there that I went along to the Army Careers Office and applied for the Royal Army Medical Corps (RAMC).

I began my training at the Army Training Regiment at Lichfield. By then I was twenty-four and considerably older than the other recruits. I found this to be something of an advantage as they were all so young and I seemed to know far more about life. I enjoyed the Basic Training in spite of being invited to spend a short time in the Unit Guardroom for having, of all things, improperly marked clothes! After Lichfield came Keogh Barracks, Ash Vale for the first part of medical training. Hard work and much to take in, but it was good fun. My first posting proper was to 16 Armoured Field Ambulance in Tidworth where the medical staff used both armoured and wheeled ambulances. When I arrived everybody, it seemed, was in Bosnia and I was soon off to join them. My job out there was to take medical supplies and drugs around to the various medical centres on the outstations. Not too demanding but it gave me a chance to see something of the countryside. Oh yes, they gave me a rifle 'just in case'. I had seen and used one of these things before on training. Happily the 'in case' bit they talked about never materialised.

After returning to the UK I was whisked off to Cyprus for a week but called back almost immediately to continue my medical training, this time at 33 Field Hospital in Gosport. From there it was back to Tidworth where, at last, I undertook my first real medical job, working in the unit medical reception station (known as the MRS). On promotion to L/Cpl it was back to Bosnia where I was sent to Brac Island as the one and only medic at the R and R centre (Military rest centre). I was kept busy here, including work on the occasional helicopter casevac. Eventually I was moved to Split where I worked at the medical centre with a nursing officer.

On returning home I was posted to 3 Regt AAC (Army Air Corps) in Wattisham. From there I did four months living in a tented Medical Centre way out on the Canadian prairies at Batus. I was then promoted to Corporal and sent to 3 Div Signal Regiment where I met my good friend Paula with whom I now share my home in Bickington. After this posting I decided to leave, spending the next three years studying Counselling in Salisbury. Over weekends and holidays I volunteered to work in Drugs and Alcohol counselling as well as assisting on a Mental Health helpline.

I now have a job with Addaction Devon Alcohol Service in North Devon where I work as a counsellor. And it was here that I met a friend, who works in probation and who is a member of the South Molton branch of the RBL. It was through him that I joined the Branch which I thoroughly enjoy.

*****

Clive Mace
40 Cdo Royal Marines. Sergeant.

I was born in 1936 in Tewkesbury, Glos, one of four: my elder brother also joined the Marines later. My father was a builder but mother stayed at home looking after us. Earliest memories were of green fields and the two great rivers - the Severn and Avon. I learned to swim here, usually safe enough but sadly we lost two friends who were drowned. School – I both loved it and loathed it. I hated the work side but loved sport for which I was made School Captain. I can remember a huge American camp nearby, just before D-day. As kids we would go along to watch and collected all manner of sweets and goodies. Then, one day, the whole world seemed full of tanks and vehicles on the move. They were off to war and afterwards everything felt very empty and quiet.

I left school at fifteen to try my hand in a local factory but gave up on day one. I had been influenced by my brother and was determined to follow him into the Marines. At seventeen I went to Deal in Kent for basic training. Next came Lympstone where we did field training and where life became harder. Accommodation were tin Nissen huts; freezing cold with just the one miniscule coke stove. When life was 'wet' there was a real battle to get clothes and bodies around what heat there was. And as for the ablution block – just enough hot water for the first few and that was that. Cold showers and shaving for the rest. Then came Bickleigh where we did commando training – tough, relentless and unforgiving. Here we grew up quickly. At the end of all this we became Marines and got our green berets, at which point I volunteered for a Cliff Leaders course at Land's End. Again hard going.

My first posting was to 40 Cdo who were in Egypt shortly before moving to Malta. From here landing craft took us across to North Africa for training where we were based just outside Tripoli. Back in Malta, we were down in 'The Gut' one evening, behaving ourselves, mind you, when we were picked up by the Shore Patrol and taken straight on board *HMS Ocean*. We sailed for Famagusta from where we were deployed into the Troodos mountains and were pitted against General Grivas and his EOKA terrorists. Personally I was involved in a number of contacts. The first I remember was when we were ambushed. The leading scout car hit a land mine and we came under fire. I was manning the bren gun in the lorry behind and gave covering fire as the lads deployed. In spite of our anti-ambush drills the terrorists got away but left one of us dead and another wounded.

The next occasion was when we were on foot patrol and were again ambushed. We were a bit luckier this time and although one of our patrol was wounded, we wounded one of them and captured another. On yet another occasion we were part of a big sweep and had cornered some terrorists. They reacted by setting fire to the forest which burned ferociously and quite out of control. We made for the high ground but the seven local forest rangers who were with us took shelter in a cave and were all burned to death. On a happier note we all learned to ski. We had to, as it was the only way of getting about the mountains in Winter. In Spring you could ski in the morning and swim at Episkopi in the afternoon. Fabulous.

On moving back to the UK I did a number of courses including a further climbing course. Eventually I was posted across to 45 Cdo who were on operations in Aden. I was then a Corporal but also a Troop Commander. Operations were in both the Crater District and in the Radfan mountains. Contacts with the enemy were frequent, both sides taking casualties. From there it was back to the UK and a Sergeants' course before flying out to Malaya and back with 40 Cdo. Straight into the jungle. We went right up to the border and patrolled against the Communist Terrorists (CTs). Again we had a number of contacts, however I was evacuated with malaria and dysentery. By this time Borneo had blown up and we were rushed to Kuching. Again it was into the jungle but this time we built a series of forts along the border with Indonesia. This time, however, it was us who were doing the ambushing and we had a number of successful contacts. But I was not so lucky and walked into a Dyak pig trap which, quite literally, speared me. I was extremely lucky to get away with it but was casevaced to Kuching.

A short time later I was sent to Oman on secondment, training Arab soldiers. I found myself with the Northern Frontier Regiment (NFR) patrolling both the desert and the mountains. During this time we had a number of contacts with insurgents, several of whom we eliminated. On completing this tour I returned to 40 Cdo where, after a damp squib of a trip up the Persian Gulf where Saddam Hussein was sabre rattling, we returned to the UK and I was posted to BRNC Dartmouth as a combat survival instructor. From there it was back to Lympstone for a further spell of instruction. Eventually I rejoined 40 Cdo but it was soon back to Oman and the NFR where we were used as a blocking force in the Jebel Akhdar mountains. We had a number of contacts here and managed to prevent the enemy from linking up with those further south.

I returned to 40 Cdo but so did my malaria – and far worse than before. In fact it brought my service career to an end, my last days of duty being at Stonehouse Barracks, Plymouth. I settled first in Bristol, working for Cadburys. Much later my partner and I moved to North Devon, near Barnstaple in the beautiful countryside just off Exmoor. I joined the South Molton Branch of the RBL in 2006 and very much enjoy the friendship and camaraderie.

*****

Ian Marchant
Army. Parachute Regiment. Lance Corporal.

Born in 1970 it started with the TV programme 'The Paras', then the book 'The Paras'. Finally a pat on the back from a proud grandfather. Tall, skinny, sixteen year-old school kid from Kidderminster, Worcestershire. Thought I was fit – wrong! Army Careers office, medical check and a short fitness test around the car park. Thirty second interview followed by the oath of allegiance and 'Sign here, sonny.'   I'm in!

Middle of eighty-seven joined Junior Para at Pirbright Guards Depot. The dreaded beasting begins! Spent six months in Juniors. Met lads who are still my best friends and we still keep in touch. Then on to Depot Para, Browning Barracks, Aldershot to join up with 534 Platoon. Beasting level rockets! But met more friends and brothers. Then 'P' Company and the real beasting – only twenty-two out of a hundred made it. Then on to Advanced Training at Brecon – here we go again, but it feels great. Followed by Para training, RAF Brize Norton and, finally, Passing Out parade in March 1988.

1 Para, Bessbrook Mill, Armagh, Northern Ireland for this seventeen year-old. Followed by 1 Platoon, 'A' Company back in Aldershot. Yet more beasting but more friends and brothers. Fort Ord, California for eight weeks came next. Big deal, I spent my lot - £2,000 in ten days on R&R. Riotous youth, they call it. My mate sat next to me in the aircraft prior to jumping. 'Walk in the park, this', he cries. 'You're pushing you luck', I tell him. Silly bugger, tripped in the port exit door. Got pushed out head first by the PJIs. Saw him at the RV in one hell of a state. Walk in the park, eh?

Moved to 3 Platoon for Northern Ireland Training then into Belfast as a Senior Tom. Waiting to go on patrol at Woodburn RUC Station. RUC patrol came in from Andersonstown. Armoured landrover followed them in as escort with two crap hats as top cover. Heard a racket in the landrover and stacks of smoke billowing out. One of the crap hats had had an ND (negligent discharge) with his baton gun. The bullet ricocheted round and round inside the vehicle, bloody nearly killing the pair of them – had our best laugh for ages.

Contact on the Ardoyne estate late one evening when we were working out of New Barnsley RUC station. Protestant attack on suspected PIRA terrorist. The Biffs were supposed to shoot out the windows then grenade the house. Grenade bounced off the window and landed in the garden where it detonated and stunned them all, so they shot up the house instead. Idiots. Needless to say none of the intended were injured. Their getaway car made off at speed and met us head on. I was with the boss in the primary team – last man in the team with the baton gun. We all signalled for the car to stop but had to leap for our lives to avoid being hit. I stood my ground and, for my efforts, got collected by the car and taken for a ride on the bonnet. I remember seeing the terrified face of the driver as I clung on to the windscreen wipers. Where I had hit the car I had smashed the windscreen. I didn't know at the time but my baton gun had bent itself around the shape of my back against my body armour. I punched through the rest of the windscreen trying to get at the driver but he had started swerving from left to right in order to get me off. He did just that at the next corner where I looked back at my team mates. We didn't hang around but opened up on the car as the Rules of Engagement said. Tracer was coming out of houses, off walls and cars – everywhere. Everywhere, that is, except the intended target which whipped round a corner and the occupants legged it never to be seen again. In spite of that we had managed to shoot up three parked cars and somebody's television set.

1992, promoted to Lance Corporal. After Ireland moved to Support Company and the

Mortar Platoon. Number 1 on the mortar from 1992-4. More good mates. Exercised in Sardinia. Jumped with the mortars. High winds and we took forty percent casualties. Del King was dragged through the RV by the wind but still managed to shout out number, rank and name to the Sergeant Major as he swept by. A good Para, Del!

Left the Army in late 1994 after seven and a half years. The peace of Civvy Street – no more beasting at last. Lost a few good mates down the years but made a lot more. See them from time to time at weddings and funerals as the years roll by. Started my own business in 1996. Joined the South Molton Branch of the RBL in 2011. Making more good friends – brothers, and sisters too. Helped the lads win the Exmoor 3030 competition that year and the next as well. Never thought I'd be beasting again and it hurts a bit more these days.

2012 went back to the WOs and Sgts Mess for the Dining Out of a few old mates who had stuck it out for the duration and who'd survived all that had been chucked at them. Miss them all like hell. I really do. 'Every man an Emperor'. 'UTRINQUE PARATUS'.

*****

Alan Marshal
Army. Royal Tank Regiment. Trooper.

I was born in 1960 within earshot of the Bow Bells – another cockney lad – in St Mary's Hospital, Hampstead. Hardly knew my father as he pushed off so I was brought up by my mother with the help of a nanny provided by the family. Mum did secretarial work in the City. Life on Broadwater Farm back then was mighty tough – gangs, guns, you name it. School was not a favoured option either – playing truant with my mates was much more exciting. At fourteen I moved to Bournemouth and had to fight my way into society there as well, literally with boots and fists due to my London background and my colour (father was Jamaican). However, almost as soon as I broke into a crowd of mates my thoughts turned towards the Army. Either that or sport as I had been made an offer to turn pro at football, and I represented Hampshire at athletics and cricket. As soon as I saw some tanks near Swanage, the Army won.

I signed on in Bournemouth then, after assessment at Sutton Coldfield (where the Irish Guards tried to poach me), I joined as a Junior Leader at Bovington. First memories were of the barber who we called 'Sweeney Todd'. I came along with a right full blown Afro-Asian hair-do and he did me just before lunch, shaving off half and then kicking me out when he locked up and went off for his grub. What a lunch break that was! My early life had toughened me so I found the 'beasting' no big deal. My sworn enemy was our Troop Sergeant who tried to break me. Tried everything but no dice. Then, on passing out, he shook me by the hand and tried to get me to transfer to his mob (The Royal Hussars). Too late, I had opted for the tankies of the RTR, but we parted good friends nonetheless.

I was posted to 1 RTR who I joined after leave, at Herford in Germany (4 Armoured Div). The camp was almost empty as everybody, except A Squadron, was in Northern Ireland. I immediately did my tank driver training: we were equipped with Scorpion light tanks (76 mm gun) and the Scimitar armoured recce vehicle with its 30 mm cannon. Eventually, when everybody came back, I joined 5 Troop, B Squadron. Early days were difficult as nobody spoke to the new boy and the vast majority of them were Scousers or Yorkies, none of whom I could understand anyway. One way out for me was sport and I represented the regiment at rugby, playing on the wing. I also played for the BAOR U-19s and in Summer I did athletics and was awarded my Regimental colours.

Workwise, training was hard as we were the Corps recce troops and deployed right up against the German border. As with all armoured personnel the real bugbear was keeping the armour on the road, well maintained and clean. Field firing was conducted both in Germany and Canada at Batus, the big training area. While over there we visited Calgary during the stampede. *Yeee-ha*! It was great, both there and further down in the Yellowstone National Park. Back in Germany we conducted range work at Soltau and up at Bergen Hohne. And, yes, like everybody else we won our spurs and other things in the fleshpots of Hamburg and further up in Amsterdam where it was even better.

Life, however, was not always fun and accidents did happen. I lost a very good mate who was killed by accident in the vehicle sheds. Surprisingly enough I never really took to tank gunnery and always opted to either drive or command the vehicle. I suppose that this might have been a throwback to the gun law I experienced in my early days. Strange really - I just don't know. At the six year point in my career I decided that I had had enough and put my cards in. I had to do a further eighteen months but left the Regiment and the Army in Herford. For a while I earned my keep as a disco DJ in Night Clubs, then moved further afield to Portugal. After this I was at a bit of a loose end for a while. I moved back to the UK, dabbled a bit in this and that, including some scaffolding work, and then, all of a sudden, came the light on the road to Damascus. Quite literally, I turned from the poacher into a gamekeeper. I decided that I would work with youngsters in Borstal or in Remand homes ie those just one step from prison.

I put my own troubled youth to good advantage and more often than not was able to break through to these troubled lads who were on the slippery slope. I did this for three years or so then moved into Social Housing for young people. This changed again when I decided to work with rough sleepers (those down and out on the streets). I'm still doing this now and really enjoy it although it can be very frustrating due to the lack of resources. On the other hand it is wonderfully rewarding when you can bring somebody back into society from the depths.

I joined the South Molton Branch of the RBL in 2007 and absolutely love it. It's a place where one can swap yarns about Service days and I have made a number of really good friends.

*****

Alan McEvansoneya
Army. Coldstream Guards. Guardsman.

I was born in 1959, and when I left school I started work as an apprentice slaughterman. I got very bored while doing this and thought that there had to more to life. So I joined the TA, the Wessex Yeomanry in Barnstaple. I really enjoyed it so decided to join the Regular Army. I signed up and was recruited into the Coldstream Guards on the same day as my brother. I did my basic training at the Guards Depot at Pirbright. I found it pretty tough going but was determined to pass out. Some of it I hated but I loved the shooting. One part of the assault course was a rope over an evil stretch of water – hand over hand swinging yourself across. I'm not sure how or why but an Irish Guardsman who was with us would always run at it, miss and, time and again, crash headlong into the water. A good laugh the first couple of times but after that he would just get in the way of the rest of us who were being shouted at and booted along by the instructors. On another occasion I was accused of being asleep at a checkpoint. Not me, I can assure you, but the Sergeant who found me, quite literally, jumped all over me. Very painful it was and not much fun, but there you go.

Six months of this and we passed out. I was posted to Windsor Castle to be the Queen's Guard. After a bit, it was not as interesting as we thought – patrolling the battlements at night was not my idea of soldiering. There were lots of ghost stories about the castle and, one night when I was walking slowly along a particularly dark passageway, I saw what appeared to be a figure moving silently towards me. Moment of panic, I'm not ashamed to say as there should not have been anyone else about. But no, it was a lone policeman and I breathed again.

After Windsor we were posted to Sennelager in Germany for Battle Training. Here we trained in a mock village, whole streets of houses and whatever else one would find in a village. Both us and the 'enemy' used plastic rounds. Plastic they may have been but still painful enough when hit. Our billets weren't up to much – they were an old German WWII 'SS' Barracks and were spartan in the extreme - cold water, bare concrete floor, walls and ceiling and barely a bed in the place. Not recommended!

This was the run up for us to deploy to Northern Ireland and now, at last, it was for real. That said, we never had much trouble but we had always to take care that we were not seen to be favouring one section of the community before the other. But then, even the quietest of streets could suddenly erupt. The terrorists, we knew, were there and were always watching us. Whenever we had to control pedestrians, we would get violent and abusive hassle from the women, especially mothers collecting their kids from school. Such language, difficult to believe, but we had to take it all on the chin and not retaliate.

I remember once we were in a traffic jam and a big digger was alongside us. After a bit the driver tried to get out but fell flat on his face onto the bonnet of our rover. Funny enough, but even then such a reaction from us could create aggro. Passing local pubs and drinking dens could be awkward, too. We used to clock those hanging around outside then check them against the wanted list. Funnily enough the scariest bit of all was going off to the airport for R and R. We would be driven by a driver with an armed escort but we would be in the back behind wire mesh in civvies and unarmed. Pretty dodgy if we ran into trouble!

After this it was back to Germany where I transferred to the mortar platoon. I enjoyed this as the job was much more interesting, especially when we worked with the anti-tanks, to light up their targets during night firing. While here we managed to get back to the UK for a spot of R and R which included some sailing at Cowes and happy times in London at the Union Jack Club.

I gave in my notice to leave the army in 1979. It had been a great experience and I was very nearly tempted to go back. For a while I was in and out of jobs but eventually became a scaffolder. It was then that I met my wife. A few other jobs came along but then disaster. I slipped a disc badly in my neck, which touched my spinal cord. It resulted in me being disabled and I am now virtually confined to a wheel chair. It was then that I joined the RBL. It's really a bit like the army, making good friends, excellent comradeship and a bit of banter at our monthly meetings.

Stuart McKenna
Army. Royal Highland Fusiliers. Sergeant.

I was born in Redlands Hospital, Glasgow in 1966. My father worked in the construction industry but, when I was just four years old, my mother left, leaving me and my elder brother of eight. Drumchapel District was, and remains, a mighty tough area – in those days gangs, drink, drugs and a number of guns were the order of the day. We had to look after ourselves out on the street from an early age, a matter that made for a lively and interesting first few years. Primary school was not bad as I had not got far to run for cover from the opposition. Secondary was passable for me also because my elder brother held sway with his boots and fists, sometimes on my behalf.

I left school at sixteen and went straight into Boy Service at the Bridge of Don. Discipline was tough; a quick thumping, or a bit more round the back of the block usually sufficed, but I knew I had to survive and abide by the rules – just get on with it. However, survive I did, passed out and joined the 1st Battalion in Palace Barracks, outside Belfast. Life came as a bit of a shock as violence in several areas continued to present problems. I joined 5 Platoon, B Company only to find my brother next door in 6 Platoon. He again made life a bit easier for me for obvious reasons, but left after six months and I was then on my own. But life looked up. We were based in North Howard Street Mill in Belfast patrolling wherever there was trouble, usually the Springfield Road or The Lower Falls. The rioting was sometimes pretty bad but the Jocks made good use of the rifle butt and the boot in and amongst the hail of bottles and rocks.

After Northern Ireland came Berlin where we found ourselves guarding Rudolph Hess at Spandau. Although we were never supposed to set eyes upon him we often caught glimpses of this strange old man as he went about his daily routine. Frequent mobilisation exercises known as 'Rocking Horse' took up a good deal of our time, as did the occasional train guard duties to the west. I remember Berlin as a wonderfully live city with a fantastic nightlife of all shades – something for everybody, literally. The city had a pace of life of its own and seemed to keep going 24/7. One amazing memory however, was of the stark difference between the wealthy, fast living west and the dull, soulless and empty east – the land of oppression and secret police.

From here it was to Edinburgh for a tour of public duties at Holyrood House, Balmoral and Edinburgh Castle. Our routine was broken by the Ambulance strike when I found myself posted down to Welwyn Garden City as a controller. But the main event by far was the Lockerbie outrage. We were called out that evening and rushed to Lockerbie where we met up with the police. Our job was the grimmest of all in that for four days we had to search for bodies and body parts. Grim and ever grimmer as time went on and the bodies decomposed, we could do little else but grit our teeth and press on – all of us coming away with dreadful memories that we'll never forget.

Next came a posting to Cambridge, from where we did two tours to Belize. Having done our jungle training we patrolled the Guatemalan border. The jungle there is dry and on one occasion our water containers broke when they were thrown out of the helicopter and we had to survive for three days on pineapples – not as much fun as it sounds, I can assure you! Then back home for the New Year to be greeted by a police knock on the door. 'Get back to your unit' was the order. I went, hoping to be included in the draft for Iraq, but was posted to a Juniors' training establishment instead. Something of a let down. After this I rejoined the Battalion in Fallingbostel, Germany where we became armoured infantry mounted in Warriors.

This tour included a couple of trips to Canada for training at Batus, and further trips to Poland. Then came Bosnia. We were deployed early in the emergency when there was a lot of shooting, both sides going for each other and very often at us. We didn't lose anybody but a number of the Jocks were wounded. My abiding memory of the place was one of a beautiful country that had been totally devastated by the warring factions, of seemingly endless wrecked buildings, pockmarked by shell and machine gun fire, and of appallingly bad roads. A terrible waste.

Then it was back to Fallingbostel to patch up and I was posted away, back to Scotland where I joined The Black Watch at Fort George in Inverness. I remained with them until my own Battalion came to take over and I rejoined them there. After this came a tour with The Highlanders – out to Fallingbostel again, believe it or not.

But time was now running out and I came home to see my last days of duty at Inverness. On leaving the army we went first to Peterborough where I began working in the Care business, initially looking after children. None too happy up there, we remembered holidaying happily in the West country and so I looked for work down here. I remain working in the Care industry, my work now centred around South Molton where we have our home. I had joined the RBL a few years earlier and switched to the South Molton Branch in 2009.

John Miller
Army. Royal Tank Regiment. Lance Corporal.

Born in Poole, Dorset, in 1982, I was the middle of three children. Dad worked in a Ryvita factory and Mum stayed at home looking after us lot. First memories of life was of me forever falling off my red bike and getting covered in cuts and bruises, much to everybody's amusement except mine. Early days at school were great, I lapped it up, in particular the maths. I enjoyed my sport, playing football for the school and athletics (long distance). The cane was always held as a threat but the old boy who displayed it simply threw foam bricks at us instead. Just before senior school, my life changed. My parents split up and Mum took us off to Wells in Somerset with her new partner who she later married. My last two years at school came to nothing as I got in with the wrong crowd. Wasted really, however the Army was beginning to loom in my mind.

I went to the Careers' Office in Taunton and chose the tanks due to a fascination I had with armour and engines. The assessment took place at Pirbright in Surrey and then came Basic Training at Bassingbourn, Cambs where we were the first batch of Junior Leaders. I found it no problem physically but the personal admin and all that cleaning of kit was a real pain. Anything we did wrong, anything at all, was punished by countless press-ups, scores of them every day. At the end of training there were sixteen of us left out of sixty. I survived OK, becoming the best shot with the SA 80 rifle. Next came Bovington with the Phase 2 training which included tank driver training.

After all this came the posting, and I was off to 2 RTR at Fallingbostel in Germany. It was a massive culture shock for a sheltered seventeen year-old lad. I was completely on my own, had never flown before or been abroad. I was collected at Hannover by the Duty Driver, who didn't want to know me, and taken straight to the Lions' Den. There, horror of horrors, I was posted into the Command Troop where all the brass worked on exercises and ops, including the CO (God to us squaddies!). We were away on exercise almost immediately, my job being to drive a Scimitar armoured recce vehicle. Soon after this we did a six month stint in Canada at the Batus training area where we were the demonstration regiment. In between units coming out for training, we got in a lot of Adventure Training ourselves including parachuting, parasailing, skiing in the Rockies and canoeing.

Back in Germany, my next big adventure was Kosovo. 2 RTR went as peacekeepers. Still in Command Troop, I worked in the Operations centre which was kept going twenty-four hours a day, seven days a week, controlling the whole regiment's activities. In and out we did a number of armed foot patrols. Memories are of a beautiful country with friendly people who appreciated that we had saved them from a grisly time. After returning to Fallingbostel it was straight into the training season where we started with individual training, such as fitness and marksmanship and worked up to full regimental deployment. Immediately after Christmas 2002, we were warned of for Iraq (Op Telic). Our heavy armour (Challenger 2 tanks) moved off ahead of us and we married up with them in Kuwait. After a very hurried redeployment the flag was dropped and we were off. 2 RTR were one of the leading regiments in 7 Armoured Brigade to cross the border. For my part I was a gunner in 17 Troop, Falcon Squadron.

Initially it was pretty quiet as we moved forward, until we got to Basra, that is, where we were subjected to RPG (anti-tank rockets) attacks and small arms fire. By this time, the enemy had abandoned much of their armour (Soviet T-55 and T-62 tanks). We remained mounted in our armour for a month and then it was out on our feet doing foot patrols. It was while we were still mounted that we lost Sgt T.C.Roberts, a very high profile casualty which the media had picked up due to the fact that he had got no body armour when he was hit. A sad loss. Our part of the operation lasted four months and it was back to Fallingbostel. I then received my tape (up to L/Cpl) as well as a posting to Bovington as a member of the Provost Staff, of all things. But I had had enough and decided to leave, my final days of duty being in Jan 2006.

Initially, I took up a job as a carpenter, building multi-million dollar yachts for Sunseeker in Poole. Then came something of a tragedy. A severe motorcycle accident saw me with a badly smashed leg and in a wheel chair, but only temporarily thankfully. It was then that we decided to move to North Devon to join my wife's family. I now work for a small vehicle restoration company which I really enjoy. In 2010, my boss (ex-Para) dragged me along to the South Molton Branch of the RBL, and it's great. I've made plenty of good chums and it's good to be able to talk about old Army days.

John Moore
Royal Air Force. Airframes. Chief Technican.

I was born just outside South Molton in 1937 and was called forward for National Service in 1958. I immediately made two decisions: first to marry my girlfriend and, secondly, to make the RAF my career. After six weeks of being knocked into shape, I was posted to Wellsbourne Mountford to join 1002 Squadron. There I found myself living out of my kitbag which didn't bode well for married life. After Basic training at Weeton, I was posted to RAF Colerne (Wilts) Transport Command. I did not qualify for a Married Quarter, so we bought a 22 foot caravan and lived at No 13 Airmen's Caravan Site.

In 1960 we were sent to Kuwait when Iraq invaded but, whilst there, the fighting stopped and I was told I was going home to go on a six week tour of South Africa. We were taking VIPs to countries that were due to gain their independence. After landing at Lagos we were ordered into the Congo (civil war) on a rescue mission. When we landed a bullet went into the main wheel tyre (just how we repaired that without any jacks is another story). We stayed at Salisbury where Mr Ian Smith, leader of Rhodesia, was made to sign the documents with Harold Wilson.

In 1963 I was sent on a Blue Missile Course at RAF Newton and then posted to RAF Scampton, 617 Squadron, Vulcans. In 1967 I was posted to the Middle East for a year and when my family joined me we flew on to Singapore, Tengah. One evening our aircraft, on return, was taxiing along the runway when it stopped and radioed the Control Tower to say that there appeared to be a log in the way. Nothing was found so the aircraft returned to the flight lines. When the mechanic got into the nose wheel he saw two eyes looking at him – two eyes plus twelve feet of body. He got out fast! After much struggling, a local civilian employed by the RAF was able to get hold of the snake's head. Finally a team of six managed to pull it free. It was taken to the Station

Hygiene Flight and fed on baby chickens. Sadly, though, it disappeared. Rumour had it that somebody rather fancied the skin.

Next, Changi, Singapore to work on the two Andovers which were part of 48 Squadron. I was just settling in when I was switched to work on the Hercules. We had a Hercules unserviceable in Nepal – a problem with the hydraulics and elevator system. Having changed the component, we had to get all the air out of the system. Job completed successfully, we returned and I duly made my report to the Engineering Officer. He passed the report on to the manufacturers and, from then on, we never again had a similar problem.

Our football team was invited to play against the inmates of the notorious Changi Jail. After a short while things turned distinctly nasty and we were hurriedly asked to leave – the only people ever to get thrown out of jail. 1971 saw me back at Colerne, the main servicing base for the Hercules. I was now a Ch/Tech and was in charge of the modification section. One of my principal tasks was flying to the States in a Belfast to bring back sections for the Hercules due to a serious corrosion problem. After our modifications the Hercules were 'stretched' to become both longer and wider.

In 1976, I was posted to RAF St Mawgan to work on the Nimrod survey aircraft. From there I was sent on detachment to Malta (Luqa) with 203 Squadron. Thence on to Iran to drop off specialists in Iraq (Basra). The idea was to survey the Russian submarine fleet exercising in the Indian Ocean. While there we were told that the Shah had been deposed. The same day I posted a card to my wife with the Shah's head on the stamp. One of the very last, if not the last, ever to be posted.

Returning to Malta, I was told I was going back to St Mawgan. This was suddenly changed to the Azores where a Nimrod was stranded. On landing, we met the Captain who asked how long it was going to take. My reply was by 1200 hrs if all went well. By 1130 hrs the aircraft was serviceable. The Captain looked at his watch and said 'I thought you said 1200 hrs'. My reply to him was that I had to get to the PX to buy a set of golf clubs for my son. But… at 1200 hrs, sharp, we were off. On the way we over flew a Russian fishing trawler re-fuelling twelve Russian submarines. With all cameras whirring, we descended to five hundred feet and got them. Russian intelligence must have deduced that the Nimrod would remain stranded for longer and they had chanced their arm – the whole of the Russian Atlantic submarine force. A few days later I was given the photo of the Russians we caught red handed.

In 1981 my medical classification was lowered which meant that I could no longer work on aircraft. I was told that I would be posted to the MOD, London but, not over keen to become a tea boy, I refused and was discharged on medical grounds. Leaving the RAF, I worked for the Post Office in South Molton until it was downgraded. In 1986, I was elected to the Town Council, the following year to the North Devon District Council and, for a short while, to Devon County. In 2007 I decided to finish with councils but, in 2011, I put myself up for re-election and was duly elected.

Mike Morgan, Poppy Appeal Coordinator
David Hadley Morgan. Gloucestershire Regiment. Private.

"No known grave".

I heard the phrase from my parents at an early age, but had never understood either the significance or to whom it referred. Also, every year on Remembrance Sunday my brother and I were called to "attention" at 11.00 and made to stop playing for two whole minutes. These were seeds sown on infertile soil. But they grew later.
The first flowering was when I discovered that the person being referred to was my uncle (father's brother). This was supplemented by learning that he had been killed at Dunkirk. Otherwise the incident was not discussed.

I did know about Dunkirk – I was keen on history. Personally I did not fancy the army. I wanted to be a naval helicopter pilot, but if I had gone into the Navy it would have been a new departure for the family. Both my grandfathers had been members of Yeomanry units in about 1900, and my paternal grandfather served in the Boer War. Later in life I became very interested in family history and this lead, in due course, to investigating what had happened to my late uncle. He was a Territorial before World War II, called up on 3 September 1939 to join his unit, 5th Battalion, Gloucestershire Regiment, who were initially assigned to guard Filton Aerodrome at Bristol.The Battalion joined the British Expeditionary Force in France on 15 January 1940.

*When the German army invaded Belgium and the Netherlands in May, the BEF were sent forward to stop the advance. The 5th Glosters reached Glabais at 0400 on 17 May, before beginning to withdraw when the BEF was outflanked by a second German attack to the south. The troops marched westwards along roads packed with refugees and were subject to frequent air attacks. By the time they reached Frasnes they had covered – on foot - 95 miles in 83 hours. Through a combination of further marching and transport, the Glosters reached Dunkirk and were then ordered south to the villages of Arneke and Ledringhem, north-west of Cassel, where they were to form part of the rearguard defending the British retreat to Dunkirk. The positions were "to be held at all costs"

German artillery began shelling the villages on 27 May and by the following day German troops had surrounded them. The Glosters were ordered to withdraw "after dark or when you can", but were delayed by strong enemy attacks. The Glosters made three bayonet charges to clear German soldiers from Ledringhem, before beginning to withdraw. They had held Ledringhem for two and a half days. The surviving members of 5th Battalion Gloucestershire Regiment reached the beaches at Bray Dunes on 31 May and were evacuated by some of the "little ships".

Through my family tree research I obtained a copy of the death certificate. It stated that Pte Morgan had died "between 28.5.40 and 29.5.40" in "France", the cause of death being "presumed killed in action". He was 24 years old.

On 18 February 1991 my wife, young daughters and I, armed with my research notes, visited Ledringhem. Having parked by the village church we walked through the adjoining municipal cemetery to the Commonwealth War Graves at the rear. The commemorative plaque reads: "Ledringhem Churchyard: The British plot here contains the graves of 51 British soldiers who fell in the later stages of the withdrawal to Dunkirk …." The Regiments represented are the Royal Warwickshire Regiment (4 names), the Gloucestershire Regiment (24 names), the Cheshire Regiment (7 names), the RASC (1 name), the Royal Artillery (1 name), the Worcestershire Regiment (4 names) and the Worcestershire Yeomanry (2 names). Eight graves are simply marked "A soldier of the 1939 – 1945 War".My daughters laid flowers on all the graves marked "unknown soldier".

Having (almost) always bought a poppy in November it was a natural step to volunteer to stand in my local shopping mall (in Hampshire) with a tray and "sell" them each year. When I retired to Devon I offered my help to the South Molton Branch, only to find that in a very short space of time I was asked to take on the role of Poppy Appeal Organiser. I have been informed that like others who hold more prestigious appointments worldwide, I can never retire from the post!
And each November my first thought on Remembrance Sunday is of my uncle, who I never knew.

* *summarized from Chapter XIX of "Cap of Honour, the 300 years of the Gloucestershire Regiment" by David Scott Daniell, by kind permission of the Trustees of the Gloucestershire Regiment Museum.)*

Clive Pearce
Army. King's Royal Hussars. Captain.

Not a Devon man, I was born in 1954, brought up in Gloucester until eleven years ago when I moved to Barnstaple with my present job. Coming from a military family it was obvious that the Army would be my chosen career. Dad served in WWII with the Royal Scots Fusiliers, then the Parachute Regiment and finally the Royal Gloucestershire Hussars. My brother began his career as a Junior Leader then went on to serve with the 11th Hussars before joining the Royal Gloucestershire Hussars.

I began military service in the Army Cadet Force before joining The Wessex Yeomanry in 1971. The next three years with the TA was a great start to Army life as I went from here into The Royal Electrical and Mechanical Engineers (REME), having completed a four year apprenticeship in 'Civvy Street'. Basic training was at Arborfield Camp where my Drill Corporal, rejoicing in the name of Cpl Perfect took one look at me and snarled, 'My name's Cpl Perfect…I am and you will be'. A charitable introduction I have always remembered. Once fully trained, my brother claimed me to his regiment, the Royal Hussars, and I was duly posted to Sennelager, Germany – my introduction to The Cold War. It was my first time abroad, I loved every minute of it and tried to drink Germany dry.

I applied to transfer to the Hussars and was told to wait until I had completed my first tour of duty in Northern Ireland. We were posted to Castle Hill Camp, Dungannon where we had an interesting and fast moving tour. My sole contribution was to be almost shot by the RUC after dropping my pistol in the town centre whilst out buying Christmas decorations. Even so my transfer eventually came through in 1977. A year later it was back to Belfast in the Markets Area. Day one and the IRA decided to blow up the gasworks: exciting enough and the start of a hard tour. Back to Germany but then home to Catterick camp in Yorkshire at the RAC Training Regiment, however I was lucky enough to be sent to Belize in Central America. That said, we spent the next six months in a tin hut with no hot water and extremely basic facilities. Close to the Guatemalan border it was patrol after patrol once jungle training was over.

I rejoined the Regiment when they were back in Germany once more at Fallingbostel, but not for long. The Sultan of Oman's Armoured Regiment was equipping one squadron with Chieftan tanks and I was posted to Seeb in Oman for two years. Time flew by and it was back to Germany yet again. I put my name down for an exchange programme with the Australian and New Zealand Army known as 'Exercise Long Look'. Lucky again, I left a baking hot Germany in July to arrive at a snow covered runway at Waiorua, New Zealand. Then Northern Ireland once again and the delights of the Maze Prison – very different, to say the least. Hardly had I returned to Germany from this tour than it was home to Tidworth. I loved Germany and relished serving there but Belize came again and, not much later, yet again. What had I done wrong?

At the end of all this, the Regiment was in Munster (Germany once more) but I found myself posted to 'C' Squadron, the Royal Wessex Yeomanry at Stroud in Gloucestershire as a permanent staff instructor (PSI). However, it was a case of onwards and upwards and I next found myself back with the Regiment both as a married man and as a Squadron Sergeant Major. Defence cuts struck and we found ourselves amalgamated with the 14/20th Hussars in 1992 to become the King's Royal Hussars and I was to be the Regimental Quartermaster Sergeant of the new Regiment. But no – obviously somebody out there didn't like me for I was off again, this time to be the RSM of the Royal Hong Kong Regiment. This was the pinnacle of my career, something I had striven for and the happiest time of my life. Sadly, the Regiment disbanded in 1995 thus I returned home with an adopted son to rejoin the Royal Wessex Yeomanry for my last six months as a regular. However, I had not yet had enough and after twenty-two years in the Regular Army and three with the TA, I rejoined the TA where I was commissioned and served as MTO.

Having had a full, exciting and challenging life in the forces, which I have enjoyed enormously over the years and travelled the world extensively, I am now well settled here in Devon and am looking forward to 2014 and my retirement from the Services. I decided to join the Legion to give me something to focus on in the future, where I will meet like minded personnel who, like me have served their country. I admire the work the Legion does for ex-servicemen young and old and feel the need to give it my support. The South Molton Branch is a mixture of young and old with a great sense of camaraderie, which makes you feel welcome from day one. I look forward to many years as an active member.

Barry Price
Royal Air Force. Administrator. Flight Lieutenant.

Born in 1944, I lived with my parents and two brothers in a very comfortable flat in Barnet, Hertfordshire. My Father was the Managing Director of a US typewriter firm and consequently there were no post-war hardships for us. In fact we had everything we could wish for, however Father was strict and we were taught the value of money and, most importantly of all, respect for our elders. It was very nearly 'Seen but not heard' Apparently there were frequent visits to the air raid shelter, an AA battery firing close by, together with the odd 'dog-fight' over the golf course and several V2 rockets. However I was too young to be aware of all that.

A recruiting presentation for the RAF at school sowed the seed for service life and it seemed that I was at RAF Cardington for attestation in no time. There being limited trades available I went, aged 16 years, to RAF Hereford for 18 months training as a Boy Entrant clerk. It was a culture shock as the degree of unremitting violence amongst the many hundreds of boys, totally ignored by the permanent staff, was traumatic.

Posted to HQ Bomber Command, High Wycombe in 1962, I was one of many clerks that scurried around the offices; buildings that were designed to look like houses from the air so as not to attract the attention of the Luftwaffe during the last war. From here Air Chief Marshal 'Bomber' Harris planned the Thousand Bomber raids into Germany. The design must have worked as the HQ was never damaged, which is more than can be said for some German industrial cities.

I was married in 1964 and a year later learned that my impending posting to BDLS, Washington was cancelled. That is when I first became familiar with the phrase 'It's all part of life's rich tapestry', when my boss followed up with news that I was posted to the Shetland Isles. No explanation was offered.

Newly married, this posting was 'unaccompanied' so my wife stayed home. RAF Saxa Vord was remote; no air strip, and no trees. The mail was delivered twice a week by boat depending on the weather; winds of 100 miles per hour were common and had recently destroyed much of the technical site equipment. Walking to work was sometimes difficult if not impossible. An airman was due for detention, and I volunteered as one of the escorts to get him safely to Colchester Detention Centre. The 'mainland' of Aberdeen was over twelve hours away by boat but it took seven hours just to reach it via 3 buses and two ferry boats. It was a one way ticket for the prisoner but we had to return the same day.

My posting to the SHAPE Paris, was another world, but interesting to work with the nationalities that make up the NATO forces. A US Army corporal friend was promoted to sergeant with 18 months service and he actually thought that I had been disciplined when he heard that I had 7 years service and was still only a Corporal. In 1971 I was selected for the Special Duties List on the personal staff of the AOCINC, Episkopi, Cyprus. Although an ideal family tour, past terrorist in-fighting was never far from the surface, and sporadic bombings in Limassol came to a head in 1974 when Turkish forces invaded and the island was again divided, Greek from Turk.

In 1977 I served with the FCO, British Embassy Brussels, with the Defence and Air Attachés. Security was always paramount especially after a shooting incident at a British Embassy in the Netherlands, followed by a bomb explosion in the centre of Brussels; where British military bandsmen were due to perform. I was escorting the band but thankfully we were delayed en route and civilian casualties were few. Tension increased when we were warned that we were under surveillance but we never learned the outcome and it was only a mild distraction from what was a very interesting and unusual three years.

In 1981 I graduated from the RAF College Cranwell as a commissioned officer, a proud moment and I am sure that my feelings would have been shared by my late Father, Sgt Sydney Price, London Rifle Brigade, 1914-1919. In 1989 I was appointed as the EO to the AOCINC HQ Strike Command, High Wycombe. Here I worked daily with senior British and US military personnel during the Gulf war. In 1994 I returned to Strike Command to effect my discharge. Many years had passed since first I marched through the gates as a humble AC1, however on this occasion I walked in and rode out on horseback after 34 years service. I gave the Unit CO a smart salute with my riding crop as I trotted out of the HQ.

There were many more postings but too many to detail here. They were enjoyable with great, life long friendships gained. After discharge I had a number of jobs but decided to try university and obtained a BA (Hons) and Masters Degree, MA, both in History. I moved from London to South Molton in 2001 and now enjoy every moment of it. There is a great sense of camaraderie between veterans and serving personnel and this is in evidence in our dynamic Branch of the RBL, which I enjoy greatly.

Denzil Priest
Army. The Devonshire Regiment. Private.

Born in June 1935 to Cyril and Lilian Priest, I found myself in the middle of a family of well known builders. I went to the local school and look back on my early life with affection – fond memories interspersed with recollections of the usual schoolboy mischief. My father first joined the Navy but then, in some mysterious way, managed to transfer to the Army's Royal Artillery, when I found myself living in married quarters at Okehampton. Having seen service at Alamein and then Greece, my father next joined the Parachute Regiment where he dropped at Arnhem, finishing the war in Germany.

On leaving school, I took myself off on further education before working as a builder in the family business. I received my call up papers in 1954 and duly reported to Alphington Road in Exeter from where I was sent to Topsham Barracks for basic training. My initial posting was to join a party of The Devonshire Regiment that was being deployed to Kenya in support of the Kenya Police. The Kenyan Mau Mau was a militant African national movement of the Kikuyu tribe whose aim was to remove the British rule and to rid their country of European settlers. In October 1952, the Governor – Sir Evelyn Baring – declared a state of emergency and the conflict raged for four years with considerable violence before gradually abating.

I found myself stationed outside Niarobi, where I spent my time patrolling both the town and the surrounding countryside. Monkeys galore and rumours of the odd leopard but nothing more sinister than that confronted us. In spite of the fact that the emergency was still in progress, my most abiding memory was of the peace and quiet and of the friendliness of the people, in particular the children. Wherever British soldiers go, children are bound to congregate, encouraged by sweets and the conversations held in two entirely different languages. At some time on the tour I was accorded the privilege of carrying the 'Bren' gun, a right b...... of a beast that took the shine off these long and wearisome patrols. Life was beginning to become boring when I and a number of others received orders to join The First Battalion stationed in Celle, Germany.

Posted to 'B' Company, I found a very different life – in particular the weather where the German winters differed markedly from the heat of East Africa. War had been over for less than ten years and the effects of the conflict were plain to see. And yet I found no animosity, the local people were, as far as I remember, remarkably friendly. My most vivid memories were of patrolling the Inner German Border where, deep in the Harz Mountains, the border cut a wide swathe through the pine forests. The sight of the electrified fence, the mine strips together with the East German Border Guards with their loaded weapons and their dogs, remains clearly in my mind. But it was a trip the Belsen concentration camp that I remember more clearly than anything else. Walking through the camp we were all quite speechless. Quite literally our mouths dried as we gazed about at the mounds of the mass graves, the extermination buildings and the strange, eerie silence.

Life was not all sight seeing, however, and I well remember the enormous exercises when The Devons, either on foot or mounted in armoured personnel carriers, supported the British and Allied armour as they practised time and again what they would do should the Russians and their friends ever decide to come our way. In 1956, The Devons received new colours, ironically just a year or two before they amalgamated with The Dorset Regiment to become The Devonshire and Dorset Regiment. September 1956 was a busy month, culminating in the parade itself when The Lord Lieutenant of Devon – The Right Hon The Earl of Fortescue KG, PC, CB, CBE, MC – presented our new Colours on behalf of HM The Queen. The Regiment remained thus until 2007 when it was disbanded, to re-emerge immediately as 1 Rifles.

Perhaps my fondest memories of service were of the sports' field. I really loved my sport, representing both my regiment and the army at cricket, football and cross country running. It was the fantastic comradeship that made it all. That and the cheap fags and booze, and the lovely long weekends away with your mates, when it was off to the fleshpots of Hamburg or wherever. Great days! I have no regrets whatsoever…I thoroughly enjoyed it all.

Demob came in 1957 when I returned to the family business, became a Special Constable and had to remain in the Reserves. The one and only time they called upon me was when some prisoners had to be moved from Exeter Gaol to two HMP Prison Farms near Witheridge. That was a laugh, but, other than that, Private Priest was left in peace. Now that I am fully retired I enjoy time with the RBL. It's a great organisation. Great people, real friendship and a wonderful atmosphere.

Ivy Rees
Army. Queen Alexandra's Royal Army Nursing Corps. Captain.

In 1939 I was born in Lambeth, London – a true, full-blooded Cockney. We stayed put throughout the Blitz and were bombed out twice, losing everything. My first memory was of being deep in a London Underground shelter, hanging upside down from my bunk bed. Later the Doodle bugs came over and we were bombed out yet again, when the bomb landed just across the street. Father was away serving with 1 Queens at the time. He was captured in Italy and ended the war as a POW in Germany. The war had its effect. I suppose I had a dose of what is now known as PTSD, which meant that for years I was highly strung and very nervous, only beginning to calm down when I was a teenager. But then I survived; I was lucky.

After leaving school I worked in an office until old enough to begin nursing. I trained at The Miller General in Greenwich, qualifying as an SRN in 1961. Almost immediately I emigrated to New Zealand on the £10 Assisted Passage scheme. I continued my training in midwifery out there. I loved New Zealand, working first in New Plymouth and then lovely Rotorua before going south to Christchurch. It was a wrench going home but, in 1964, I decided to return. However, there was a problem – in order to complete the Part II of my training I had to deliver twenty babies. Try as they might they couldn't find the last mother until 0300 hrs on the day I sailed at 1000 hrs. She delivered and I made the boat, just! I heard that I had passed by telegram when en route between New York and Southampton.

I then did a course on Sick Children nursing at Sheffield. By now I had thoughts on the Army and went along to the old BMH Millbank for an interview. They accepted my qualifications and I was commissioned as a Lieutenant. Aldershot came next for the unavoidable square bashing, officers or not. 'Get those dozey idle arms swinging properly – ma'am'. Then it was to the Louise Margaret (known fondly as 'The Lousy

Mag') as a military midwife although this was, by now, my least preferred choice. Among my patients were Mesdames Ridgeway and Bligh (wives of the celebrated Atlantic Rowers).

After only six months I was posted to BMH Rinteln in Germany. Situated on the River Weser, Rinteln is a beautiful town, surrounded by lovely countryside. The people were friendly and I really began to enjoy myself. My job was to assist running the Children's ward which I eventually took over when the incumbent left for further training. Although specialists, we all took our turn at Night Duty in both A&E and on the General Wards. We had little to do with the British Military except for accidents on training and the roads. The one exception was a well known (now defunct) Highland Regiment who seemed determined to take on everybody and everything in sight, and getting themselves into a fine old mess along the way. Diplomacy prevents me from telling you which Regiment it was, but the inhabitants of Minden knew them as the 'Poisoned Dwarfs'.

And, yes, romance came along as it usually does. I used to love my rugby and was an avid supporter of the Hospital team – cheering them on to win the BAOR Cup, in fact. He, one of the team, and I met at drinks after the game. One thing led to another and for a while we had a marvellous time but the draconian Military rules came between us. Fraternisation across the ranks in those far off days was not permitted – it was totally and utterly forbidden - so, sadly, after a few glorious months we went our separate ways.

Berlin I remember well. What a place and what a train journey to get there! The day we arrived there were riots for it was the time they shot Rudi Dutschke. I was caught up in the worst of it, but all of a sudden found myself very much on my own. Everybody else, except me that is, had seen the water cannons coming on to the scene and I took the full blast. Then came Check Point Charlie. Told to do nothing at all provocative, we found ourselves taking photos of Russian soldiers as they snapped away at us. Much hand shaking, waving and fraternisation before the authorities broke it all up.

Life in BAOR was fun and the work rewarding, my main concern being the children. I have to say that, in spite of all my years of experience and exposure to it all, one never gets hardened to the plight and suffering of sick or injured children. My last day of duty was at Rinteln and I emerged from the BMH as a retired Captain and wended my way back to the UK. I decided to leave as I wanted to go into Families' Health and Welfare. I did this happily for many years ending my working days as a tutor at Guy's Hospital in London.

Looking back on it all there are many fond memories. We knew Devon from holiday visits and moved down here in 1995. And why the RBL? It's a great charity and I thought it would be nice to be part of it so I joined in 2008. There's a very friendly atmosphere in the branch. Smiles everywhere and many members have now become friends.

Tony Reed
Royal Air Force. Aircraft Fitter Electrical. Corporal Technician.

I was born in South Molton in 1939. My grandfather, Harry Reed, served in the Wessex Regiment during the WWI and saw service in France. My father, Reg Reed, served in the Royal Engineers during WWII, serving in France, Holland, Germany and Palestine. My brother, Michael, served in the Royal Signals for twenty-one years. As such I can claim to have strong service connections. At school I lived for my sport, eventually representing Devon schools at soccer but later switching to rugby.

In 1957, after basic training at RAF Bridgenorth which, incidentally, I found easy due to my fitness, I was posted to RAF Khormaksar in Aden, serving as an Air Electrical Mechanic on 84 Squadron working on Valettas. Here I met John Stacey who was also in the RAF, and Ron Cree, who was with the Cameron Highlanders, both from South Molton. John is also in our branch of the RBL here at South Molton. Some memories of Aden remain clear, such as the time I was given a rifle and fifty rounds and told to board a plane for Dhala. This was a wild and woolly spot close to the Yemen border and deep in 'bandit country'. As if to prove its point, we came under fire as soon as we landed – young Reed had been blooded. Another, happier, memory was when we met up with a bunch of US sailors in the Rock Hotel and helped them celebrate July 4th in a robust and noisy fashion that went on a bit. On a more sombre note, however, I and a number of others happened to be in an Italian restaurant in Steamer Point when it was blown up, resulting in the loss of a number of off duty Royal Navy personnel.

1958 saw me posted away to RAF Sharjah in Trucial Oman for fifteen months, a cushy number in comparison to Aden. What was amazing was Dubai Creek where we went shopping. Then it was just that, a small, still backward town on the edge of the smelly creek up which dhows crept, but what has since been transformed into one of the world's greatest and most opulent shopping malls where state of the art is the norm. After this it was back to the UK for a posting to RAF Colerne, working on special installations, in particular radio and radars, also sophisticated and highly classified electronic surveillance and monitoring equipment. From here I moved to RAF Disforth to join 60 MU. There I was employed as a Technical Author writing up electrical modifications to various aircraft on the fittings of SRIMS.

Then, in 1964, came Cyprus for five months serving with the UN at RAF Akrotiri where we worked mainly on helicopters. After this came Singapore, based at RAF Tengah, serving with 60 Squadron on Javelins for a time, before moving on to Hunters for a further nineteen months. While at Tengah I played rugby for the station and I well remember when we beat our sworn enemies – RAF Changi. Celebrations began at once, ending up with serious partying in Raffles. Come midnight and my time to report back for duty and I was gloriously and helplessly 'trapped', the result of which was a rapid posting, first to 20 Squadron and then to Labuan in Borneo. Such is life, but no regrets. Being a single NCO meant that one could be moved around fairly frequently and, while here, I saw spells of duty at Butterworth, Kuching, Bahru and Hong Kong.

All good things must come to an end and 1967 saw me back in the UK at RAF Colerne once more, this time working on the C-130 Hercules. A year later and the dreaded redundancies struck and, although I tried to stay on I was made redundant as rank and trade had become superfluous, or so I was led to believe. I returned to South Molton where my parents ran 'The Mitre' pub in nearby Bish Mill and it was here that I first met the young soldier who is now our branch Chairman. Far more importantly, though, it was here that I met, Mary, my wife. I managed to find work locally based on my profession in the RAF as an Electrical Engineer.

I had been intending to join the Legion for sometime but finally signed up a number of years ago and joined the South Molton Branch. I must admit that I really enjoy it, in particular the great camaraderie, the friendly atmosphere together with the banter and good humour

Keith Rodulson
Royal Air Force. Ground Radar,Wireless.
Warrant Officer.

Father left the RAF before I was born in 1946 and then rejoined in his old rank and trade, so I travelled around with my parents. During those years I went to school in Cheshire, Yorkshire, Germany and Blackpool, leaving at fifteen to join the RAF as a Boy Entrant at RAF Cosford. Boy Entrant training was like a military boarding school for boys between fifteen and eighteen. Passed out aged sixteen as an Air Radar Mechanic and posted to RAF Marham, Norfolk to work on V-Bombers (Valiants). Spent my first Easter there as part of the back up to the civil police as the CND were trying to break in and get to the V-Bombers. Whilst I was there the Valiants were scrapped as all the Main spars (which hold the wings up), had metal fatigue. Ended up in the Telephone exchange for twelve months. I also had a detachment to RAF Chivenor when I met my future wife at South Molton. Warned for a posting to Aden, but before I could go the Government decided to pull everyone out.

Eventually posted to RAF Waddington to work on Vulcans for a few months and then on to Station Flight where we looked after all the visiting aircraft, everything from Spitfires and Javelins, to Beverlys and Dakotas. Serviced Lancaster PA474 before it joined the Battle of Britain Memorial Flight. Moved to RAF Locking in Somerset, which was the RAF Training School for Ground Radio and Radar trades where I was trained as a Ground wireless fitter. Whilst there I got married to Ann and our first son, Andrew, was born.

My first overseas posting appeared out of the blue, to Bahrain, unaccompanied for thirteen months. Originally went to RAF Muharraq, then moved to *HMS Jufair*, which had the Joint Communications Centre. Although with the Navy – no tots of rum! Posted back to RAF Chivenor, which pleased the family and then, in 1970, posted to Cyprus for three years accompanied. Lived at RAF Akrotiri where our second son,

Stephen, was born. Whilst there, my sister and her husband, who was in the Army, was posted to Episkopi, and then my parents to Akrotiri as father was still in the RAF. The whole family there at once!

Left Cyprus before the invasion and posted to RAF Henlow, Bedfordshire, where I was a member of the Ground Radio Installation Squadron (GRIS). GRIS members travelled the world but, apart from a six week trip to RAF Gan, I never went more than sixty miles from Henlow. There I was promoted to Sergeant and warned for a posting to RAF Masirah, which was another staging post in Oman, for nine months unaccompanied. I arrived just as the fighting had finished further down the coast at Salalah. Life there was hectic – just two aircraft a week.

Back from Masirah to RAF Cosford, another training unit, but as a member of the permanent staff working in the Telecomms School. 1978 posted back to Cyprus, this time to Episkopi to 12 Signals Unit. Ann and the boys joined me after three months. More restrictions, as this time the Cypriots were trying to recover from their war. Back to UK, this time to RAF Rudloe Manor in Wiltshire to 6 Signals Unit working underground in an old stone mine. Promoted and posted to RAF Abingdon, Oxford. A fairly routine staff job but I did manage some travel.

Back to Cyprus yet again, to 12 Signals Unit, this time just with Ann and Stephen as Andrew had joined the RAF. Promoted once more and back to UK. Soon we were on our own as Stephen had decided to join his brother in the RAF. On his 18th birthday Ann flew back to UK to surprise him but the RAF flew Stephen to Cyprus. So…Ann flew out one day and back the next. Decided that we would drive back to UK, as we would probably never have the chance again, via Greece, Yugoslavia (Balkan war had not started), Austria, Switzerland and Germany to visit Andrew who was stationed there.

Back to Henlow on a staff job, not much travelling here either. Whilst on holiday I had a phone call out of the blue from HQ. Did I want a posting to Germany? Did I! Needed an answer by lunchtime. Didn't take long to decide, but I had to go to Italy for six months training at a NATO Radio school just south of Rome. Really rough and a great base to explore Italy. I even learned to like pasta. Ann managed to come out for two weeks holiday. Posted to Rheindahlen to work in the basement of the Big House in a NATO slot, in charge of a detachment. One of the best jobs I ever had as my boss was two hours away. Stephen, by this time, was also posted to Rheindahlen and lived just two streets away.

Posted back to RAF Locking, looking after instructors and students on postgraduate courses. After my post was taken over by a civilian, I became assistant to the Wing Commander Engineering until my final promotion and posting to RAF Oakhangar in Hampshire which is the RAF Satellite Communications Unit. Stayed there for just over three years, through the millennium when everyone thought that all the satellites would come crashing out of the sky. Absolutely nothing happened.

After demob, Ann and myself moved back to South Molton which we always said we would do and, for some time, I worked for Eaton Aerospace. Andrew is still in the RAF and has just come back from Afghanistan. Stephen was medically discharged from the RAF and, after a long illness, passed away just before I retired. In July 2001, I joined the South Molton Branch of the RBL.

*****

David Sewell
Royal Air Force. Aircraft Fitter, Airframes.
Junior Technican.

The Summer of '69; Bob Dylan was going to the Isle of Wight, The Archies were in the top ten and I was in the RAF. No 1 School of Technical Training, 216 Entry Comet Flight. 216 Sqn flew Comets at the time so we were adopted by them, an association that continues to this day, hosting our reunions at RAF Brize Norton.

Sunday morning was obligatory church parade, but not for us all. Colin Myers was Jewish so was excused. Marching back up the hill after church behind a band, he would merrily blast us with Led Zeppelin from his record player by the window. We would be bussed down to the airfield for our aircraft handling training. There we learned the art of marshalling from our instructors, who did their best to run us down as they chased us about in their Piston Provost aircraft. The armourers were in the next door block so we teamed up with them to make bazookas which fired tennis balls. Our targets were the 'sootys' (engine fitters) on the other side of the parade ground.

October '71 saw us pass out to Monty Python or Liberty Belle and posted to the 'real' air force – in my case RAF Chivenor. Where's that and what do they fly? North Devon, Hunters and lots of them. At first I was put in the hangar on a servicing team. Dead boring, but had to do a spell on the 'flight line' to learn all about it. (Yippee!).

I managed to stay out there for most of my time at 'Chiv', also doing time with the target towing flight, visiting aircraft flight and air experience flight. Sat on the pan one afternoon with my engine man, waiting in our slot for our last aircraft to return. We didn't notice how long we had waited till the line boss came to tell us not to wait any longer. He had failed to make it....

The run to Machrihanish with the outboard drop tanks full of fresh fish on return – the brass stopped our game when a seagull was swallowed by the engine as he took off on the way home. We had all these two seat Hunters T7 and they would often go with just the pilot. What a waste! So, a quick word with the boss and off I went for kitting out in a 'G' suit, helmet etc, then survival training with the dinghy at the Braunton Road Motel, and finally, the ejector seat drill. After all that I wasn't going to let anything go with a spare seat, even the Meteors were fair game. At that time Harold Wilson had a house on the Scilly Isles, not too far for a really low ground attack.

Many other memories – endless mobile patrols on Guard duty, chasing rabbits in the bomb dump, and picking mushrooms before breakfast. Getting 'jankers' for something or other and cricket when they were a man short. Not forgetting the month long detachment to Gibraltar. Met Sue in '73 and married in '74 as well as posted to RAF Brawdy when 'Chiv' closed. I had applied for an overseas posting and, not hearing anything, went to the General Office to chase it up. They told me that I was posted to Cyprus but when the Turks invaded it had been cancelled. Would I like to go to Hong Kong instead?

Our VC10 landed on Kai Tak's infamous Runway 13 at 0800hrs local time on 1st Jan 1976. Married quarters were right by the 'Chequer Board (where the incoming aircraft turned) made for a very happy Bunny. We met some local Chinese people through a friend on the camp, who took us under their wing, taking us with them on picnics and places that we would not have got to otherwise. Sue had her wisdom teeth removed in the BMH and upset the Army surgeon by discharging herself because he kept referring to her as 'wife of J/T Sewell'.

We adopted the Squadron dog, a Japanese terrier called Mick. He ate frogs, loved the Ghurkas in the camp next door, but detested the Chinese who took a short cut through the compound. The food was amazing, everything from the housing estate next to the camp, street food in the markets to Russian vegetarian restaurants and MacDonalds. President Markos of the Philippines borrowed Concorde to take his wife to Hong Kong to buy shoes the day before it was due to arrive on a round the world sales tour.

I spent a lot of time doing liaison work with the local aeronautical engineering firm HAECO that did the deep servicing for the Wessex, so familiarised myself with the other aircraft that were in for maintenance. We shared the hangar with the Royal Hong Kong Auxiliary Air Force who were also happy enough to let me scrounge as much flying as I could manage. Two years soon passes and it's back to earth with a posting to RAF Abingdon and the Field Repair Squadron (FRS), or 'Smash and Crash' as it's known. FRS was a travelling unit so I could be at RAF Benson taking rust out of Nimrods, Conningsby re-riveting the Lancaster, Valley changing the wing tanks of Hunters, or St Mawgan putting a Canberra back together.

Working on lumps of metal that didn't fly soon lost its appeal, so in '79 I became Mister again. My last effort at Abingdon was to put a metal stake right through the airfield electrical ring main that carried power to the approach lights, runway lights and taxiways, just one day before the annual airshow! Funny, but they did seem to be sorry to see me go.

*****

Eddie Smith
Royal Air Force. Safety, Survival Equipment. Senior Aircraftman.

Born 3rd Feb 1942 in Great Ryburgh, North Norfolk. Abandoned at birth so lived with my grandparents. The Germans bombed the local malt factory and I was evacuated as a result. Hand of fate selected me to go to Brisbane, Australia. Bombed by the Japs this time, who sank some shipping in the harbour and had a go at us. Escaped to Sydney. Got sent to a sheep station in the outback where us boys were separated from the girls for education etc. Aged eleven I moved to Perth with a family and from there to Melbourne. Finally back to Sydney again.

I made enquiries with help from the family I was with, to get back to the UK. I knew nothing about my parents or where they lived etc. Got back home and met everybody who were total strangers – my parents were, by now, divorced and neither wanted to know. No affection at all and on my own again. Still had a few weeks at school and joined the Air Training Corps which I loved. 1959 I joined the RAF before getting 'called up'. I was sent away for the 'square bashing' – some of which I actually really enjoyed! Applied for a job as a Safety Equipment employee only to be told I had to sign on for twelve years. Once I had done this I was told the job was unavailable. Was offered a Cooks' course (I can't even burn toast) or the RAF Police until my preferred job came up. Down to Netheravon in Wiltshire for the course, then offered a job as a Dog Handler. Really enjoyed it but the Safety Equipment job became vacant so it was off to RAF Weeton, Blackpool. After training it was RAF Wattisham – loved the job and the lads I worked with. Went up with The Black Arrows in a Hunter. Fabulous! Then came RAF Changi, Singapore.

Wonderful posting – extra cash, tropical kit and life in the Orient. Did many jumps – 106 in all and joined Far East Survival School. Sent to Borneo and N. Malaya; learned to live off the land. Never seemed to be at home. Got caught out once in a security drama in Singapore during the Communist uprising. No shots fired but bricks were thrown. One hit me. Avoided the mob but lost my watch. Next stop was training on an Oerlikon Gun waiting for the Indonesian Migs to attack us. No such luck and was sent back to the UK. Where to? Wattisham again.

A chance meeting got me sent back out to Changi once more, would you believe! Took on Jungle Survival again, main task was to rescue downed personnel, both military and civilian. Saw the world out there – Hong Kong, Japan, Gan, Burma and Thailand to name a few. I was young, fit and lived my life to the full. Once in Borneo I went into the jungle on my own. Veered off the track, found a waterfall and had a good swim. Looked up and saw an armed man. 'Who the bloody hell are you?' I laughed at him but a couple of rounds over my head sobered me up. Heard later there was an SAS patrol in a cave above the waterfall. On the way back I stumbled across the wreck of a Japanese Zero fighter with the skeleton of the pilot inside. Nobody knew but later confirmed by the SAS.

Did a night jump over the jungle canopy and came down in the trees. Unknown to me it was a very tall tree indeed and when I released myself the ground was a long way down. Fell and damaged my spine. Three days on the deck before they found me. Hospital – UK – and discharged from the RAF. Managed to persuade them to keep me in but no more jumping. Eventually I did make my way home doing a stint in RAF Akrotiri, Cyprus on the way. 1970 now and at Wattisham went up with the Red Arrows. Even better than the last time! RAF Chivenor next with a spell or two in Gibraltar to protect the Rock from the Spaniards who kept buzzing the place.

Demobbed about 1972 and had to start work for a living. Lived initially in Barnstaple, eventually moving to South Molton, close to work at the Chipboard Factory. When I was about fifty my world was shattered. I collapsed – went to hospital only to be told that I had a severe muscular disease. I would never walk again, work even, so from then on I have been confined to a wheel chair. I miss the RAF dreadfully as well as my many civilian colleagues. It was in South Molton that I learned about the RBL. When they moved to The Coaching Inn, I could attend in my chair.

This has opened up a whole new life for me. It is a great gathering of ex-military folk with the same attitude to life. Both young and old with heaps of memories and loads of tales to tell. I would like to include in my happy life that my good lady, Jean, has looked after me and encouraged me all the way. This in turn has made me realize what real life is really all about. If I can somehow help somebody then I will do it. That's the RBL spirit. After all how can I forget those who fought so hard for our country, allowing me and Jean to have done everything we have managed to do?

*****

John Stacey
Royal Air Force. Radar Mechanic. Senior Aircraftman.

I was born in 1938. My father, a career policeman moved to east Devon in 1939 and after World War Two we moved to Barnstaple then Exmouth where I was educated at the excellent Colyton Grammar School. On leaving school I started work in a radio shop learning to repair valved radios, and black and white televisions, later moving to Rediffusion Exeter to distribute wired radio and television programmes. At this time I was also studying a part time course at home on radio engineering.

In 1956 with National Service becoming inevitable I joined the RAF on a four year engagement. My first taste of RAF life came at RAF Cardington, home of the gigantic balloon hangers. Energy sapping 'square bashing' came next at RAF Padgate. Never did I want my mother so much as when I stepped, or rather fell off that bus onto that hallowed tarmac, with the Corporals shouting at us. I thought I had been transported to Hell and during the course I think I was proved right. However I managed to qualify as a marksman with the Lee Enfield 303 and also the LMG (Bren Gun), relics of WWII

Next came the Number 2 Radio School, Yatesbury to train as an Air Born Radar

Mechanic to work on 'gear' installed into the then 'A' bombers - Victors, Vulcans and Valiants. Happy days by rail to Calne, with its factory famous for its pork pies. Cold winter nights on guard duties in creepy generator rooms or tending to the CO's mushroom crop, are best forgotten. Next was RAF Honington to work on Valiants and the 4 minute warning readiness against the 'Ruskies'. I dread to think what would have happened if we were ever put to the test. I was never sure whether my country needed me or I needed my country.

My posting to Aden was a shock to the system. My first response was 'where the hell is that'? I found out after a cruise around the Bay of Biscay with a small company of Gurkhas and some very secretive and detached RAF Russian interpreters. Arrived at Steamer Point in January 1958 and my God, was it hot? I moved later to RAF Khormaksar working on transiting Service and civilian aircraft. And best of all, a Bristol Sycamore Search and Rescue Helicopter Flight, but to this day I have never been up in a helicopter. Highlights of the tour; flying as an armed guard to the Yemeni border to collect and return a very pregnant Arab princess to hospital. Being surrounded, once landed, by some very serious tribesmen, straight out of the 'Arabian Nights' armed with ancient guns who intended to join us. We persuaded them that it was not a good idea, just. In later life I had helped to deliver my son but this Arab lady was much too close to delivery for my peace of mind. As an ambulance cadet I could fold a bandage and CPR but I must have missed maternity classes! Whilst in Aden I came across Tony Reed from South Molton. Low points of the tour was seeing the poverty of back street Aden and Mombasa where a cardboard box for a shelter was worth more than gold.

I flew back to 'Blighty' in a Hastings, 'prop' job, my first time being air sick. If you are in boat, at least you can lean over the side. My final posting before 'demob' in September, 1960 was at RAF Gaydon OCU. This was the end of my military service apart from 23 years of being a reservist. Later, after missing the notice in the national press, I found that I could apply for the GSM and Bar which up to the time I joined the RBL has lain in it's case.

As a civilian I joined J P Williams (Radio) on TV service and wiring South and North Molton for television prior to the opening of Huntshaw Cross. Then BBC2 and colour TV. WOW! One day I walked into the local Post Office and spotted the young lady later to become my wife. Marion and I married in 1963. Marion's father, Sam Wright, an ex-army PT instructor worked for Ern Chanter, baker, who is now probably one of the Legion's oldest members. I worked for two local businesses before, at the age of fifty, I set up my own Radio/TV and communication business, retiring 15 years later. One aspect of my life I should mention was the part-time work for SSAFA, helping retired service people and families, even once assisting a retired German soldier through his Embassy. My main interest is now family and hobbies. I am a licensed 'Ham' radio operator and can be called upon when required for emergency communications. I must not forget my son and daughter, both married and in senior positions in their companies. We are very proud of them both and our one lovely granddaughter. As well as being a member of South Molton RBL I am a life member of the Royal Air Force Association, the Bomber Command Association and the 7 Squadron Association and Aden Veterans who selected me, accompanied by my wife, to represent the association at a Garden Party at Buckingham Palace in May, 2012. It was a great honour and a privilege to be present at such a grand occasion.

*****

Mike Strong
Army. Glosters. Warrant Officer 2. Royal Engineers.

NATIONAL SERVICE!!! I was born in 1935 but that's where it all started, two years full time and three and a half part time. I suppose I was fortunate; I had friends who had done their time and said, 'You've got to get in there and get some fun out of it'. So…I duly reported to Depot Glosters on 5 July 1953 and away we went. Not fit, more a couch potato, I struggled hard with the PT, the obstacle courses and the cross country runs, and the dreaded Pokey Drill (Shoot to Kill exercises). I lost my rifle once but the Platoon Commander got blamed as he had moved it and forgotten about it. Great!! But the ten weeks passed like lightening and I was off to the Infantry Clerks Training Centre at Chichester.

Posted back to the QMs, the man himself was the cause of all the trouble so I was moved on to a Rifle Company with the tag 'Not for Clerical Duties'. Here we had fun building ranges up on the Fylingdale Moors – but, caught in bed after reveille and it was up to the top of the hill at the double – in pyjamas too, so they could watch you all the way. Swearing brought you two hours in the petrol store or guarding the Ammo Dump. Had the fright of my life on guard one night when – pitch black and dead quiet – came a ghastly noise. The IRA were climbing over the wire so they were. 'Fall in the guard'. 'Who goes there? Who?' A sheep, you bloody fool – just one solitary, stupid sheep entangled in the wire. While there we were told off for Kenya so it was back to the Depot in Gloucester. Hooray…no more CSM 'Jimmy'

Loftus, or so we thought. Yet there he was waiting for us at Gloucester. He never liked me anyway, and certainly not now. Got his revenge by making me his example to the recruits of how not to do it.

That was the end of the Regular bit so I took the Queen's Shilling as a TA soldier and joined 5 Glosters. Moving around with them was too complicated so I transferred to the RASC and became a Despatch Rider in the exalted rank of Lance Corporal. I considered riding about without 'L' plates a bit close to the mark and told the instructor so. It was not meant to be a joke and he didn't laugh. Glaring at me, he strode away to the office and returned waving a piece of paper and yelling like a mad thing, 'Get that bloody bike out, you…you've passed your test'. Simple as that.

Marriage came next so, needing more money, we moved to London where I volunteered for the RMP. On hearing that 'they didn't take pygmies' (I was 5'7"), I joined the Gunners, 459 Essex HAA (Heavy Anti Aircraft to be precise). After promotion to Bombardier it was off to camp with 459. I was made the OC's driver but never saw the man as car sickness kept him out of the way. Spare me! Life moved on and it was the following year at camp when I, minding my own business, was warned off for Dinner in the Sgts Mess. I had made the big jump at last. After a year in this exalted rank we moved back to Bristol to join a unit that was destined for disbandment under the cuts. Change again, this time to the Royal Engineers – yet another cap badge.

The first camp I did with them was at Ripon. Here at last, I thought, I would see life with the modern army. One glance in the stores put me right. 'Obsolete – for ACF use only' and 'Obsolete in 1945' was stamped everywhere. Furiously we boxed it all up and drove it over to the Ordnance Depot. The simple solution there was to remove the copper, pile everything into a heap and drive a bulldozer over it all. Eventually life improved and we were re-equipped, first with WS C45 Radios and finally the Clansman.

During my service with the TA (a total of twenty-one years) I attended a mass of courses here and there, including a number at the Royal Military School of Engineering (Signals Wing) and qualified as a Regimental Signals Instructor. Eventually further promotion came my way and I became Squadron Sergeant Major. During my last two years with the Sappers, my eldest son went through the ACF and somehow got me involved. They were kind enough to offer me a commission, and it was in 1977 that I relented and was commissioned as a 2/Lt. The penalty was automatic discharge from the TA as 'you can't be an officer and an Other Rank'.

I served in the ACF for almost twenty-two years as a Detachment 2 i/c, a Detachment commander and, on promotion to Captain, as a Company 2 i/c, before finally making it to Company Commander in the rank of Major. Working with the ACF is hard, dedicated work as one has to do everything oneself – preparing the programmes, lectures and running the training, but I can honestly say that I have never regretted a minute of it. And as for my forty-three years in uniform? I've never had any doubts that I have done the right thing.

We moved to South Molton in 2008 and I joined the RBL soon afterwards. I enjoy the camaraderie in the local branch, and the monthly meetings are excellent.

*****

Albert Tester
Fleet Air Arm. Airframes and Engines.
Naval Aircraft Mechanic First Class.

Born in 1941, I joined the Fleet Air Arm in 1958, and went to *HMS Condor* in Arbroath, Scotland. First up were swimming lessons in a very cold pool of sea water which, had it been fresh, would have frozen. It was a great incentive to learn quickly. My training was as an aircraft mechanic-Airframes and Engines and upon completion I was posted to *HMS Sanderling,* Arbroath where I worked on Sea Hawk and Sea Venom aircraft.

In 1960 I was posted to my first ship, *HMS Centaur*, Portsmouth, which at the time was not even in the water. However it was not long before it was out of dry dock after maintenance and refit. Sea trials completed, and having found my 'sea legs', we were off to the Mediterranean to carry out exercises with the US Navy.

June 1961, Iraq laid claim to Kuwait as a province of Basrah. The aircraft carriers *HMS Centaur, Bulwark* and *Victorious* were dispatched to the Persian Gulf as conflict looked imminent. Fortunately a war was averted. Returning to Portsmouth for engine room repairs, the ship suffered a loss of pressure in one of the pressure pipes and killed five of the crew, one of whom was a good friend of mine.

Next port of call was Malta which was a first for me and I became familiar with the notorious street known as the 'Gut' where bars and other things lined both sides of the street and were the downfall of many a young sailor boy. It was the practice to drink in every bar up and then down the street. The Spinning Wheel bar was infamous for the rather mature females, well past their 'sell by date' who would gather there. They were renowned for exposing themselves in public for the price of a drink. It was a wise man that was quick to purchase wine for them on the strict understanding that their modesty was preserved at all costs - even under the influence of drink it would not have been a pleasant experience.

On one occasion whilst ordering a drink in a similar bar a rather large sailor came across to me and asked if I was Albert Tester. My first thought was guilt followed by self preservation. Had I done anything wrong, and was he likely to rearrange my face? I was honest and said 'yes' and much to my surprise he said he was my cousin and had heard I was on board ship. Another celebration followed.

Going ashore at Singapore meant consuming much food and alcohol ending up in the infamous Boogie Street. Here all sorts of things went on including gatherings of 'Ladyboys' as they were called, young men who, to the unwary, could easily be mistaken for very pretty females and often were. It was customary for new crew members to be introduced to them. Many a young sailor who thought his luck had changed went off with one with a smile on his face only to return the next day a much wiser man!

A scheduled trip to Japan was diverted to make for Kenya and the flooded areas around Mombasa. We were not pleased and took out our frustration in Aden where a seafront club was damaged when much of the furniture and most of the crew ended up in the bay. The skipper was not amused. We finally reached Mombasa where our doctors and medical staff were flown by helicopter to help with the flood victims.

Whilst at anchor the sea was full of sharks and we used to watch the cooks throw the waste over the side to feed them. Whilst trying to attend to my duties to man the rescue boat during 'Flying Stations' I slipped off the rope ladder into the sea. An experience that necessitated a high speed exit.

During 'Flying Stations' at sea, the deck was crowded and very noisy with all the jet aircraft 'running up' and, regrettably on a couple of occasions, a member of the crew got sucked up into the intake of the aircraft. A very unpleasant incident which demanded that a small crew member, suitably laced with tots of rum, climb into the intake to remove the body. Needless to say it was not for me, rum or no rum.

In 1965 I was posted to RAF Changi, Singapore where I was attached to the Naval Support Unit who were responsible for the main servicing of aircraft for the carriers in the area. The aircraft were flown into Changi but the operation to recover them to the ship, now in dock, was to tow them back by road. A team would ensure that the folded wing did not come into contact with electricity cables en route. Late at night and with drinks taken, poles were missed, cables disrupted and villages plunged into darkness.

This was the last year that Communist Guerrillas were active in Singapore, but our sentry duties at the airfield were still thought to be necessary at night. We were armed with a .303 calibre rifle and five rounds of ammunition. The question arose as to whether I would challenge a heavily armed band of marauding guerrillas with automatic weapons. I just wanted to be invisible.

In April 1968 I left the Navy.

*****

David Tomkinson
Army. Royal Engineers. Lance Corporal.

I was born in 1959 and grew up in a small mining village in Nottinghamshire. When I was eleven, I lied about my age to get into the Army Cadets which had sparked my interest in military life (the joining age supposed to be thirteen). During my final year at school we went on a visit to the local coal mine - an early work experience programme - as there was not a lot on offer in the area at that time. It was all happening over two thousand feet down and about three miles out, and seeing the men working a 4 ft. high coal face convinced me there and then that the Army and fresh air were for me.

As I was under eighteen my father refused to sign the joining papers for me unless I joined a regiment which would give me a trade on to which I could fall back on after leaving the Service. Dad suggested that I follow him and my elder brother into the REME, but at Sutton Coldfield selection centre, the recruiting Sergeant told me about the joys of becoming a combat engineer with the REs. On asking what they did he said, "Blow fings up an' play wiv bridges and fings like that". My eyes widened.

"Really?" "Yeah," he replied. "An' there's mines an' booby traps, an' bloody great earf movin' machines, an all. D'yer wanna borrow my pen?" I was in!

After training, I was posted to 38 Engineers at Ripon in N.Yorks. From there, as part of the Strategic Reserve, I was to see many far off corners of the world, quite often at the drop of a hat – 'pack your kit, you're off to Cyprus in the morning'. After four years of this I was posted to 33 Independent Field Squadron RE based in Northern Ireland (the only unit on constant active service in the whole Army, we were told. Apparently even the SAS get days off). I arrived in Antrim in Jan 1981, a couple of months before the hunger strikers started dying. Our job in Belfast, as a Scoobie team (1x armoured shovel loader and 1x16 ton dump truck) was to keep the streets clear of barricades to allow ground units to get around the city. An article I kept from 'Soldier' magazine at the time stated that, in a four month period, our unit shifted 67 buses, 126 lorries and 325 cars from the streets, all of which had been hijacked and set on fire to create barricades to deny access to the Army and RUC.

These operations were invariably carried out in the presence of a bunch of infuriated locals. It was during one such op that my team was parked in a back street off the Falls Road, waiting to be called forward to clear a barricade, when we noticed a crowd congregating at the far end of the street. When they were about fifty strong they began to advance down the street towards us, screaming abuse and hurling stones. As we were but four in number, nerves began to fray. It was not until they got close that we realised that they were all women. At that time rumours abounded that Republican women liked nothing more than to hack Very Important bits off British squaddies. Great! I tried reasoning with a tiny, scrawny female, who I presumed to be a ringleader. She was, and shrieked at me announcing that I would never be a father. She meant it, every word, the evil hag. More abuse, more stones and, by this time, a group of their men folk were at the back egging them on. One charmer made a grab for my rifle. I pushed her away and ordered my team to cock their weapons. Hysterical rage now rose to new heights, encouraged by the men behind them.

Moving slowly backwards in face of that mob, I can honestly say that I genuinely began to fear for our lives. They meant business, real business, no doubt about it. In the weeks leading up to this incident we had taken numerous rounds from snipers, not to mention the countless petrol, acid, nail and blast bombs, and we had been involved in several riots. Yet nothing in our training had prepared us for this. The mob continued to push us back, right up to our vehicles when, without any warning, they suddenly disappeared, leaving us alone and bemused. Looking back, I can only assume that their bold aggression was due to their belief that we were never going to open fire on a group of women. However, a street suddenly emptied often heralds the arrival of the snipers (out of the frying pan…). Mercifully our friendly sniper had other business to attend to that day, and we were left to get on with our own. In two years of duty in Belfast that one incident was the one that had the most profound psychological affect on myself and my colleagues.

I finished my time in the Army serving with 32 Armoured Engineers in Munsterlager in Germany, where we seemed to spend an awful lot of time painting tanks. Since leaving the Army, my journey through life has taken me to Cheltenham, London, Hampshire and, for the last fifteen years, to South Molton with my wife, Pippa, and my two daughters Lizzie and Sophie. And I'm glad to say that I'm a happy member of the South Molton Branch of the RBL.

*****

Bob Turner
Royal Navy. Able Seaman.

I suppose you could call me a true Westcountryman, having been born in Bere Regis, Dorset back in 1923. My family later moved to Bournemouth where, after leaving school at fourteen, I was taken on as an apprentice cutter for a carpet fitter. My pay for a forty-eight hour week was the miserly sum of 2/6 (fifteen pence in today's money). On reaching eighteen I reckoned that I could better myself, and in 1941 went to Portsmouth where I joined the Royal Navy. I did my initial training at *HMS Shrapnel* at nearby Portsmouth.

I then moved to Pwllheli in North Wales for gunnery training at the shore-based training establishment *HMS Glendower* which had been built earlier by Mr Billy Butlin and which, after the war, became famous as a Holiday Camp. After this life became serious and, later that year, I was posted to Scapa Flow where we were involved in coastal defence. Soon afterwards I was posted back to Portsmouth where I joined the fleet as an anti-aircraft gunner. I remember one occasion when, redeployed for an exercise, we were told that our new skipper was to be none other than Prince Philip.

North Atlantic convoys followed and for the next eighteen months I was continually at sea. Action came often and harshly: numerous vessels on the convoys were sunk by U boats or aircraft. In one particularly memorable action, a US Navy cruiser, just two ships away from our own in the convoy was bombed and sunk resulting in the loss of all hands. Watching those men going down was a dreadful sight. I will never forget the appalling weather conditions that we were subjected to when the seas were mountainous, and when the rigging became thick with ice during the winter months. I remember that the food was awful, dull and always the same, with the living conditions both wet and cramped.

Despite the conditions the morale and camaraderie amongst the crew was incredible and I will always remember my dear mess mates and friends. Wonderful men. Truly an experience which seemed to pull us through during those dark and often terrible days.

Author's note.
When we spoke to Bob he was very frail. His mind was apt to wander and he frequently became confused and disorientated about what he was trying to remember. Furthermore, dragging the more harrowing memories back from where they had lain for so long was, for him, an intensely emotional experience. We decided, therefore, to let matters rest; further details surrounding the wartime life of this grand old man will thus remain undisturbed.

Glen 'Wally' Walton
Army. Commando RE. Warrant Officer 1.
Regimental Sergeant Major.

Born in 1970, I had wanted to join the Army from as early as I can remember. I had a pretty normal upbringing, loads of outdoor activities with my father and brother, camping and lots of hill walking. I began with the Cubs, then the Scouts and finished up with the Army Cadets. As a family we would spend the majority of our holidays and a lot of weekends in the Lake District and from an early age my father would drag us up some mountain or other. Helvelan and Blencathra were our favourites.

I joined the Junior Leaders Regiment at Old Park Barracks in Dover on the 18th June 1987, a few days before my last exam at school. I left school early as I wanted to get into the Army asap, and sitting the last exam would mean waiting another term before joining. At sixteen and a half, patience is non-existent. The Junior Leaders was an ideal start to many Army careers; a full year to learn the ropes and routines of life in the Services has definitely stood me in good stead. Having completed a year at Dover and passing out, I progressed with the same troop of lads to complete Combat Engineer Class 3 training – bridge building, watermanship, demolitions etc. Plenty of days being run ragged, or so it seemed.

My first memory of Plymouth when posted to the Squadron to attempt the Commando course, was walking through the gates of Seaton Barracks and asking the Guard Commander where the Commando course was living. Myself and another lad were told that we were late and that, right now, the course was running out of camp past us. I cannot describe the utter panic that took hold. It took about two hours for the matter to be resolved: we were, in fact, not due to start until November, so we were actually about five weeks early. I will never know how I completed the Commando course. At eighteen I weighed in at around nine and a half stone wet through and, although I was fit, I was carrying no fat or reserves. Also, being vertically challenged, the six foot wall on the Tarzan Assault Course was something else again.

The overriding memories of the thirteen weeks on the course were of being constantly shattered, forever washing our kit (the dhobi), eating everything whenever we could (we had shares in KFC) and taping my body and feet with zinc oxide tape, some of which stayed on for the entire course.

I remained in Plymouth until 1996 when the squadron re-located to Chivenor in North Devon. During that period I deployed to Belize, Canada, Brunei, the Falkland Islands and many times to Norway. The tour in the Falklands was a fantastic time, culminating in a two week Adventure Training expedition, trekking in Patagonia in the Torres Del Payne National Park. We flew over to Chile in a twin-engined plane which was re-fuelled in mid air from 45-gallon drums. Very nerve wracking, so it was. Most memorable moment in the Falklands happened during a violent storm when the roof of the bar blew off and crashed through my bunk while I was sleeping. I managed to get into the corridor stark naked only to bump into a couple coming the other way. I don't know who was the most scared, the female seeing a naked bloke covered in plaster dust or me having the roof cave in.

I left 59 Commando in 1997 when I was posted to the Army Training Regiment at Bassingbourn as a Troop Sergeant and spent two years teaching recruits. Following this I returned to 59 Commando as a Troop 'Recce Sergeant' and later as Recce Troop 'Staff Sergeant' after completing the All Arms Parachute course. Deployments to Bosnia, Brunei, Belize, Norway, Oman, Egypt and, finally, Afghanistan in 2002 followed. I deployed to Bagram Airfield Afghanistan with 3 Commando Brigade Reconnaissance Force and ended up manning several observation posts out in the mountains.

In January 2003, I was posted to the Civil Affairs Group and was sent to Kuwait to prepare for the invasion of Iraq. We crossed the border with a multi national group with 15 Marine Expeditionary Unit into Umm Qasar. Contact with the enemy was made on the first morning. What followed can best be described as a firepower demonstration, all the way from small arms, anti tank, M1 Abrahams to a Harrier with a 500 lb bomb engaged the targets. At one point a couple of UK vehicles passed between us and the opposition. Following these adventures, I instructed at the NATO Tactical CIMIC course in Italy dealing with the classification of damage to buildings and infrastructure.

I next joined 11 Field Squadron as the Sergeant Major just before deploying to Iraq on Op Telic 9 for a seven month tour. At that time, our bases in and around Basra were being constantly attacked by rockets and mortars. Quite hairy! Probably our biggest operation was the planning for and demolition of the Serious Crimes Unit police station on Christmas Day 2006. I then moved to 23 Engineer Regiment and deployed to Afghanistan on Op Herrick 8 as their RSM. Here my job was to tour the regimental area checking out the many FOBs. Following this came my last posting in the Army, when I was posted to the Export Support Team which supports UK Defence companies in the export market. Living nearby, I joined the South Molton Branch of the RBL in early 2012, shortly before leaving the forces that October.

140

Paula Watson
*Army. Royal Electrical and Mechanical Engineers,
Adjutant General's Corp. Corporal.*

I was born in Singapore in 1970 into a big Army family. My father was then serving in the Royal Electrical and Mechanical Engineers (REME). My grandfather had done so before that, as had my two uncles. I'm, thus, a true 'Army brat'! Throughout my early life I seemed always to be on the move, 'following the drum', as they say – UK, BAOR, Hong Kong, Cyprus to name but a few postings. Early days were a muddle in that I was never able to settle and was constantly changing school but, looking back on it all, I learned more about life and became far more worldly and street wise than most kids of my age.

My first attempt to join the Army, when I was just seventeen, ended in rejection as I was too much under weight. By then we were in Plymouth and I took a number of local jobs while eating like mad and playing a lot of sport. Once the clothes had got tighter, I tried again and was accepted into the REME (one of the earliest intakes of females accepted into anything other than the WRAC). I was sent to the WRAC Centre at Guildford which I found pretty tough going. Yet it held none of the great mysteries for me that it might have done, due to my strong military background. From there I went to the School of Electrical and Mechanical Engineering (SEME) at Bordon, Hants for trade training as a Craftsman (Mechanic). My first unit posting was to 7 Signals Regiment in Germany where I made many good friends some of whom I am still in touch with. And it was from here that I did my first operational posting to Bosnia.

The war had just finished and we went as part of IFOR, a multi-national force, consisting of us, Americans, Germans, French, Dutch and several other nationalities. My job was that of a mechanic repairing what are known as 'soft skinned' vehicles ie vehicles with canopies and not the armoured variety. We had very little contact with the local population but those we did meet seemed friendly enough – no doubt delighted that the horrors of war were over. I was there for a year and then it was back to Germany and from there back to England to 3 Field Workshop REME at Tidworth. Kosovo came next. Similar in many ways to Bosnia, we were in a remote spot billeted in one half of a factory, the other half working away doing what factories are supposed to do! I returned to the UK for just ten days and it was back to Bosnia again. Same old job – keeping the vehicles running.

I started off in Split North Port then moved on to Banja Luka, again working in the vehicle repair shop. The tour included a short spell in Sarajevo where we noticed a tremendous improvement compared with the earlier battle-scarred city of a few years back. Restrictions were lifted and we were allowed out to restaurants and shops – the food was delicious. On moving back to England I was posted to 1PWRR (The Princess of Wales' Royal Regiment) based in Tidworth. They were an armoured regiment, armed with the tracked Warrior and I spent my time in the B Shop looking after the soft skinned vehicles.

Then, believe it or not, it was back to Kosovo yet again. The same job as before but, here too, the situation had improved immeasurably. We could get around and saw a good deal of the beautiful country. The tour lasted for six months and it was back to Blighty – just in time to be warned off for the Firemen's strike. Charming! We were despatched to Woolwich and my job, as usual, was to make sure that the dear old Green Goddess fire engines could get themselves in and out of the barrack gate. 1PWRR were off to Canada for training with armour at Batus on the vast training area – a chance to really stretch out and go for it with the whole armoured battle group on the move together.

At this point I decided to make a change as I had spent enough of my life working underneath vehicles and getting covered in oil. I applied for a clerical job in the Adjutant General's Corps (AGC) and was accepted. I did my training and was posted to HQ 3 Div Signal Regiment, working with 202 Signal Squadron. While here I did four months in the Falklands, based on the airfield some twenty-five miles from Port Stanley. I loved it down there; the scenery and wild life were marvellous and we could take trips out to see the battlefields and were able to pay our respects at the Military Cemetery.

It was a great trip but I had put my cards in by now and, soon after returning home, I left the Service. A great friend of mine was living in North Devon, at Bickington just outside Barnstaple and I moved down. Both of us are now members of the South Molton Branch of the RBL. The meetings each month are fun and I have made a number of good new friends.

Margaret Watts
Evacuee. Former Branch Secretary.

I was born in January 1932 weighing a mere 2lbs, and my mother was told I needed to be christened within an hour as I was not expected to survive any longer. What the doctors did not know was that I, like my older sister, Catherine, was a redhead, born of redheaded parents, and their parents and siblings were also fiery redheads....just to add to this my surname was then Scarlett! This was changed years later when I married and became Margaret Watts.

The family lived in SW London and at the start of the Second World War, as there was a likelihood of children from London being evacuated to other parts of the country for safety, our lodger arranged for me to live with his parents near Cardiff, South Wales. This turned out to be one of the best times of my life for my health improved with the cleaner air and I was looked after very well. I am still in touch with family members.

My new 'family' consisted of 'Mum and Dad' John and Addy, their daughter Mary, her fiancé Jesse and younger brother Ieuan. John and Ieuan were both miners and every Friday I was despatched to the pit gates to collect their weekly wages which I felt was a great honour to be trusted in this way, as I was only 7 years old. We lived in a terraced house in a long road and to go to the shops, a journey I had to do every Saturday to collect the shopping, I had to climb one of two steep hills. It was often a struggle and one day being so thirsty I drank a bottle of vinegar but was none the worse for it!

I made friends, learned to ride a pony, which I sometimes rode to school when staying with that particular friend overnight, and did reasonably well with lessons, passing my exams when that time came. I often got the cane mostly for talking in class and, if I mentioned this at home, I got another to remind me not to misbehave again! I soon learned not to say anything after the canings.

When the bombing of London eased and peace was anticipated my parents decided it was time for me to return home. It was really exciting as I had not seen them since leaving for Wales, four years earlier. I attended a school virtually at the end of my road, however the London Education people would not accept the result of my Welsh exams and I had to sit them again - these were much easier.

However the 'doodle-bugs' were still in evidence. They were flying bombs that had a very distinctive roar and, once the engine stopped, it would glide silently down to earth, a few yards or even several miles, you had no way of telling. I was returning from school when I heard the roar of these horrible weapons and it was at the end of the road, engine roaring and I started to run when the engine cut out. I just about got to my front door when it swooped and sucked the glass out of every other house in the street. Had I been living next door, I would have been fine, but unfortunately I got the full blast and remember crawling upstairs screaming to my Mum that I could not see. The other doodle-bug travelled about 3 miles further killing 10 people when it landed on a Convent.

My Dad had died of cancer the month before having had 14 operations in seven months. I was 12 years old and from then for the next three years was completely blind. I had numerous operations and left with sight in just one eye. As a result I am petrified of unexpected loud noises such as balloons bursting, thumping desk tops and the like. I immediately go into 'trauma' crying for several minutes and during that time have no idea where I am, who I'm with or what is happening to me. People who know me and this situation just wait for me to recover. I am left with a thumping headache which lasts approximately a fortnight. All this happened when I was a child, and still lives with me.

Later I moved to North Devon, and travelling to Spain on holiday I met a lady, Kathy Young, from South Molton and after a long chat we became good friends. She mentioned that she belonged to South Molton Branch of the Royal British Legion and, as I only lived 20 miles away, she invited me to attend one of their monthly meetings. That was in 1992 and I have been attending ever since. I subsequently took over the job of Branch Secretary and only relinquished this post at Christmas 2011. Something I have enjoyed doing and have made some good friends within the group, and I hope that I shall be able to continue membership for several years to come

Bill Webber
Army. Royal Artillery. Gunner.

I was born on 26th February 1932, living initially at Factory Row, South Molton. After attending local schools, I left aged fourteen to serve a five-year apprenticeship as a carpenter at Sanders saw mill, Mole Valley. However this was never completed for, with only three months left to do, I was put on a job that took me out of town and I could not get back to attend evening school.

I was twenty when I received my National Service papers and I duly reported to Oswestry, Wales where I joined the 59th Aster Training Battery, Royal Artillery as a Gunner. I was fully kitted out but promptly relegated to camp-cleaning fatigues! Eventually I was drafted to Regimental Headquarters, 23 Light Anti Aircraft Regt in Lipstadt, Germany. Here I was assigned to the Quartermaster's Leave Kit Store. This, in spite of the fact that I pointed out that I had been in the Army as a Gunner for a whole year but had never actually been introduced to an artillery piece. Neither had I ever been on parade. However, life seemed to be an easy ride so I didn't make too much noise.

Somehow, but I could never tell you how, I was posted to the Sergeants' Mess as a barman. I paid for my food in English cigarettes at two pence a packet, and my accommodation was free. My uniform, as such, was a smart civilian suit. My first instruction from the Mess Sergeant was that it would be bad form if ever I was to refuse a drink. I pleaded that I was teetotal and was promptly ordered to keep a full glass of coca cola handy, and to always look grateful when it was bought for me. It really was a cushy number. There I was, practically a 'civvy'; nothing whatsoever like I imagined life in the Army would be like. And, what's more, I never had to draw my pay, and was even given a certificate which told whoever bothered to read it that I was fully qualified on the range with various weapons. Crazy, for, were the truth known, I had never been near a weapon of any sort. And then, as a final straw, when

I was due to be posted back to Blighty for demob, I had had to report to the Unit Paymaster and explain why my pay had accumulated quite so much. What a to do – Gunner Webber, so says I, must have scared the Russians witless.

On getting back to England, I took employment with my old firm Sanders saw mill but, as a Reservist, I was obliged to serve a further two years in the Territorial Army (TA). In the end I managed to serve for seven years at the South Molton Branch, training at the Drill Hall in North Street. And it was here at last, believe it or not, that I spent countless happy hours training on the artillery pieces that I had never once set eyes upon when I was facing the dreaded Warsaw Pact in Germany. This included live firing on Salisbury Plain and small arms marksmanship on local ranges. I have to laugh at the fact that it was only when I was out of the Army that I was doing a job that I had been paid for while serving. Anyhow, I thoroughly enjoyed it all and even became a small arms Marksman.

The following part of my life will be more familiar to the people of South Molton and North Devon, principally for my close association with the Royal British Legion (RBL). I have now served in the RBL for almost sixty years and this includes working closely with the annual Poppy Appeal since 1955, later becoming Principal Organiser in 1975. Later still, in 1984, I became Parade Marshal and then, in 1995, I was elected to become Branch Chairman, a post I held for fifteen years. But there was more to my life in that I became closely involved with a number of charities and for the last twenty years or so have become associated with fund raising for the South West Children's Hospice, Cancer Research, the North Devon Hospice and the Lions' Club. I am still a strong supporter of the RBL and regularly attend Branch meetings – to keep an eye on the young!

The Branch Chairman writes:
Bill is far too modest a man to tell us that, over the years, he has raised literally hundreds of thousands of pounds for these charities, all in his own time and at his own expense. Time and again he would give up several evenings a week to drive out to some function or other in order to raise funds. Furthermore he used his expertise as a carpenter to make toys for children which were then sold by him in the town market or at car boot sales. For over forty years this modest and unassuming man has dedicated his life to enriching those of others less fortunate. Throughout this period he has been most ably supported by Margaret, his wife, who has been a leading light in the Ladies' Branch. It came as no surprise, yet brought delight to so many of us, when it was announced in the 2012 New Years Honours List, that Bill was appointed MBE, a distinction that he carries in his typically modest way.

Bruce 'Tug' Wilson
Royal Navy. Submarine Service. Leading Hand.

Born in Harlow, Essex in March 1970, we later moved to George Nympton near South Molton. Strong service connections, my great grandfather joined the West Yorkshire Regiment in 1881, then volunteered for the Essex Regiment. Under the command of Lord Wolseley, they struggled in vain to relieve Khartoum. He left the Army in 1893. My Great Uncles were all Royal Navy during WWII. My Grandfather joined the Scots Guards during WWI but got booted out, only to rejoin with the Royal Flying Corps. My father was a Captain in the Merchant Navy, so I suppose it was inevitable I would join the Forces in one capacity or another.

I left school at sixteen in 1986 and, shortly after, went to New Zealand on my own, living and working on sheep farms and with shearing gangs. Upon my return, I started in the construction industry, tarmacking, before joining the Royal Engineers in 1990. Unfortunately, due to getting bound over to keep the peace for a year, it was a further year before I actually joined them. During this period I met my wife and we had a baby girl. Things had now changed somewhat, but feeling obliged to carry on, I left for Gibraltar Barracks, Blackwater, Camberley. Although injured, I managed to pass out from basic training where fifty-four of us had started but only seventeen passed out, with just fifteen on the parade ground. I continued with my Combat Engineer training but, due to a combination of injuries and trying to support a young family, I left the Army and returned to tarmacking. I tried several times to rejoin but all reenlistments at that time could only join infantry regiments. A friend suggested I fill my time by joining the Territorial Army – 'D' Squadron, The Royal Devon Yeomanry – which I did and spent about four years with them before joining the Royal Navy.

Whilst tarmacking on one particularly horrible day, a lorry driver jumped down from his cab with his RN sweatshirt on. He drove his father's lorry whilst home on leave. His very first words to me were, ''Ere, you wanna join the Royal Navy?'' To which I replied, 'Yes, I do. Never considered the navy before'. The next day we happened to be working in Exeter and I took the whole gang along to the Recruiting Office and made enquiries. Needless to say I was the only person anywhere near half serious about actually joining, and I was invited back for tests etc. A Warrant Officer had asked me what I wanted to do in the RN and now, aged twenty-eight, I knew that whatever it was it would have to be something completely different. I therefore suggested I was interested in the Submarine Service, whereupon a beam of light seemed to fill his office and a broad grin crinkled across his face!

I joined *HMS Raleigh* in January 1999 and begun ten weeks basic training plus another four weeks of Seamanship. The RN training was a far cry from the Army but the discipline I had learned was still there, so I was always selected as Class Leader throughout this period. I passed out from *HMS Raleigh* and was drafted to *HMS Dolphin*, Gosport for Submarine training. *Dolphin,* however, was a bit different to the Navy I knew at this point. We were greeted by a salty old Submarine Coxwain who gave us a pretty informal introduction, but warned us that if we were ever late for 'both watches of hands' (first parade), our excuses had better be pretty darned good. Several lads were late, returning with hard won trophies of bras and G-strings to support their stories to the Coxwain. The old sea dog would smile knowingly and that would be that.

My first patrol on a submarine was a baptism of fire aboard *HMS Tireless*. We made it as far as Sicily then suffered a major failure of a weld on the primary loop of the reactor cooling system. Eventually, and due to other faulty equipment, we couldn't make enough water to replace that being lost from the leak, and the order came to shut the reactor down. It was then decided to steam back to Gibraltar on the surface using diesels. *RMS Diligence* would shadow us and we went down to a skeleton crew on board the submarine with only essential and experienced personnel staying behind due to the uninhabitable conditions on board. I then found my name on the list! Later the Coxwain saw me and asked if I was happy with that. I replied 'yes' and he told me he had only picked me because I made him laugh. Great!

I spent my ten years submarine career on T-class fast attack boats and conducted many sneaky beaky patrols which I'm not allowed to talk about. We carried out numerous SF operations which were always interesting, making a point of nicking all their Gucci equipment. After one operation, an SBS S/Sgt asked for all their equipment back but we, of course, had no idea what he was talking about. 'Bloody submariners', he announced. 'Every time we come aboard these things we lose the lot'.

I left the Royal Navy in 2009, achieving the exalted rank of Leading Hand…twice, after being busted back to AB for threatening to marlin spike a Petty Officer who was a seriously obnoxious little man. I now work for a Norwegian Seismic Surveying company as a Seismic Observer. We work five weeks about and conduct surveys worldwide. I still live in South Molton with my wife of twenty-two years, and have

wo children and a little granddaughter. I was encouraged to join the South Molton
Branch of the RBL last year. A good decision!

*****

Charlie Winter
Army. 7th Worcesters. Corporal.

I was born in 1922 near Wichenford, Worcestershire and was brought up by my
grandparents. I never had a formal education as I had a severe head injury when
I collided with my teacher's car outside my house. I was in hospital for a long time,
twelve months, but I could not remember anything about it. When I returned to my
old school I could not read nor write and I was told very firmly to go back home and
to stay there. So I did and simply helped my grandfather around the house
and garden.

My grandparents were not at all pleased when I decided to join the Army as they had
lost two sons in the First World War. However in 1939, and much against their wishes,
I volunteered and was enlisted into The Royal Berkshires at Oxford. When I came to
sign on, as I hadn't proper schooling, I just marked the paper with an 'X'.
The recruiting staff could hardly believe their eyes but they still took me on!

After completing my regular training I transferred to the 7th Worcesters and moved
to the Westcountry, employed initially in loading munitions onto bomber aircraft
near Newquay. Following this came a posting to Northern Ireland, then I was back
again to Lincolnshire before going on a convoy for Durban, then on to India. I arrived
at Bombay and then the route led me to cross the Brahmaputra by steam-propelled
paddle steamer, then onwards and eastwards towards the Indian-Burmese border. By
this time I had been promoted to Lance Corporal and had been given charge of the
famous 'Bren' gun. Jungle training in and around Dimapor did not amount to much
but the jungle was very hot with the intense heat where temperatures rose up to and

beyond 100 degrees. This made our conditions worse, together with the daily tropical downpours which caused much sickness amongst the men.

The 7th Worcesters, members of 5 Brigade along with 2 Dorsets and The Cameron Highlanders were destined for the battle of Kohima. I was now a Corporal but we never had any real idea just what lay ahead for us. For us and my mates in the front line it was the horrific battle at close quarters. (A battle described by the historian A.J.P.Taylor as second only to Stalingrad for its sheer ferocity. Ed) Most of my memories are of the horrors of the battle itself and they remain with me so very vividly even to this day. I remember well having to survive on the so-called 'chocolate' iron rations for days on end, for sleeping rough on the jungle floor, of the clouds of mosquitoes, of the total lack of any form of hygiene, of the desperate water shortages and the sheer physical slog of living and operating in the mountainous jungle where the peaks rose to more than a mile high with steep steep-sided ravines which made crossing them very difficult if not impossible.

And then there was the enemy. The Japs were cunning, ruthless and as tough as nails. They fought with everything they had, you see it was a terrible disgrace to surrender and they simply died where they stood. They set wicked booby traps and they tied snipers into the tree tops. Combat was at close quarters, so close that the enemy were often no more than a few yards away. We could hear them talking. It was a question of the rifle, the bayonet and the grenade. No quarter was expected and none was given. You had to fight like madmen to survive and the dead lay all around with the stench of rotting bodies everywhere. We did what we could to recover our own dead, burying them as decently as possible and marking the spot with the dead man's rifle driven into the ground, held fast by the bayonet and with his helmet sitting on top of the butt. We had no time to do more – that would have to be done by somebody else later.

Author's note.
Memories of so many friends gone, of the dreadful conditions and the sheer ferocity of it all are hard to bear and Charlie, strong man though he is, can not bring himself to speak about it. Even so, shining through this darkness are just one or two small shards of light. Such as the time when he delivered important documents to Field Marshal 'Uncle Bill' Slim, such as when a rogue bull elephant walked silently by, inches from them, as they lay sleeping on the ground, such as the concert when the young and glamorous Vera Lynn sang for them and Charlie found himself in just the fourth row back. Imphal came after Kohima but for Charlie it was the end for he went down badly with malaria and was evacuated to the tented hospital at Dimapor.

Back to Blighty was, for me, aboard 'The Empress of Scotland' which shortened the journey home by using the Suez Canal. My final days were in Aldershot when, in spite of tempting bribes by the pre-release staff for me to remain a soldier and amass a fat pension, I decided that I had had enough. Initially I found work in Cornwall, first in the China clay industry and then building concrete pre-fabs. But it really was very dull and for years I worked as a driver for a haulage firm, before ending my working fe back in the clay industry once more – this time as a pump operator.

joined the Burma Star Association soon after leaving the Army but it was not until 1uch later that I turned towards the RBL, first in Newquay and later in Bude. I have ow settled in North Devon and attend the South Molton Branch meetings as often as can. It is the warm friendship which I enjoy most, that and doing whatever I can to upport the Legion in all that it does.

*****

Iris Wide
Sister, daughter and widow of those who served.

3oth of my brothers were in the Navy, Jim (see photo with me) as a tail gunner in the Fleet Air Arm; Harry as an Able Seaman. Jim did continuation training, first in Winchester, then in Scotland and eventually he became a navigator. He was sent to Ghana flying seaplanes, then to Freetown, in an Albatross which was forever breaking down, and on to Cape Town. From there he was sent to Ceylon Naval Base flying Avengers on submarine patrols in the Indian Ocean. He told me that he found warfare exciting at first but, as combat dragged on, he just concentrated on surviving. After being demobbed, he joined a Channel Air Squadron. However this was disbanded by Harold Macmillan, just as he was about to become a Warrant Officer.

Harry tried to join the Navy at fifteen but was found out. He finally joined in 1944 as an Able Seaman on the *Delask Cove*. He saw a good deal of action, went to Hong Kong, Brisbane and Darwin. But at some point, (I believe) he was involved in rescuing men from the sea – pulling dead and dying young men of his own age from the water. When he finally came home, he suffered for years from Post Traumatic Stress Disorder. He shook so badly that he could not feed or wash himself. He never really recovered, and what had been a handsome, popular young man, gradually became an emotional wreck.

My father's story began with him running away to sea in 1909 aged fifteen. Being a Devon man, the sea was in his blood and he joined the Merchant Navy. The first wee of WWI his ship was shelled and sunk just off the coast of Zanzibar. Survivors were machine gunned in the water and my father had shrapnel wounds all over his body and head. But he was an excellent swimmer and survived until the native boats came out to help him and the other survivors. He was taken to a German Mission Hospital where his terrible wounds were treated with great care. But the piece of shrapnel in his head could not be moved and left him blind on that side. As a child, I remember he had a jar in which he kept the pieces of shrapnel that used to emerge through his skin every now and again. At the end of his life, when his mind was clouded, he spok fluent German and spoke well of the Nuns who cared for him. But he never went to sea again. The name of the ship that sank the *Pegasus* was the Konisberg.

My husband, then a young Dutchman, was picked up off the street, one Summer's day. No chance of going home to get more clothes or to tell your parents. He was sent to an aircraft factory in Poland as a slave labourer. He had to endure a Polish winter in the Summer clothes he was wearing when they picked him up. His shoes worn out, his feet were wrapped in old newspapers and rags until a German overseer (an amputee) brought him some of his own shoes and socks. Then sent to France – Hesdin in the Pas de Calais – better working conditions and Austrian officers. Escaped to join the Resistance but was arrested by the 'SS'. Made to stand all night with his hands above his head while being interrogated. But the 'SS' were looking for a Frenchman and my husband was so Aryan with blond hair, blue eyes and a Germanic name of Werner van Wezel. After three days in prison they let him go, just in time to avoid being deported to a concentration camp in Germany.

When France was liberated, he joined the Canadian Forces as a scout. Worked up to the Belgian border and was arrested by the Gendarmes as his papers were out of date. Went on into Holland and was immediately called up by the Dutch Army. Joined the Zeeland Regiment. Took part in the battle of Walcheren where he saw many Canadian dead. Later conscripted into the Dutch East Indian Army. Sent to Indonesia where there was much hard hand to hand fighting. Suffered badly from Malaria and was repatriated to Holland but he continued to suffer from nightmares and malaria for the rest of his life. He was a brave man, his only anxiety being to meet again the men he killed in battle. The Almoner of the clinic helped him to find peace at last.

My own first experience of WWII was running down the path in pitch darkness, noise and fear all round our Anderson shelter. One evening a bomb fell between our house and our neighbour's. They were all killed. Our house had every door and window blown out but we were safe. Our school was a mile from Filton Aircraft Factory and it was badly bombed on two occasions while we were at school. The first raid killed 108 people. Both my father and brother – home on leave – helped pull the victims out and lay them in the Parish church.

Later, I lived in Flanders for fifty years and went often to the battlefields and cemeteries, also the Last Post at the Menin Gate. All so moving and sad. Langemark, Tyne Cot, Zonnebeke, places of utter misery, but peaceful now. The saddest of all is a little graveyard at Deper. On the walls are the names of thirty-six young children. How their mothers must have grieved for them. Other walls inscribed with thousands of names of those who have no known grave.

I look at the rain soaked poppy wreaths on the cold November day. I think the raindrops are the countless tears shed by so many, for so many. There are not enough poppies in the world to hide the criminality of war. There are not enough tears to wash away the eternal grief which war brings to us all. If only mothers ruled the world, warfare would cease forthwith. Will we ever learn?

Author's note.
It is fitting that Iris's story is last in the book, as it is a deeply moving tale of how one family can suffer so much through war. Her story and particularly her final paragraph, we believe, sums up the tragedy of war and acts as a lasting memorial to those loved ones who gave their lives for their country. May it also concentrate the minds of those who might be tempted, in the future, to commit our Armed Forces to further conflict.

Glossary of Military Terms and Slang

AC1	Aircraftman First Class
Addoo	Arabic for enemy
AOCINC	Air Officer Commanding in Chief
ATS	Auxiliary Territorial Service
BDLS	British Defence Liaison Staff
Beasting	Very hard physical training
CPR	Cardiac Pulmonary Resuscitation
CTCRM	Commando Training Centre Royal Marines
DS	Directing Staff
DUKW (Duck colloq)	WWII Amphibious Landing Craft
EO	Executive Officer
FOB	Forward Operating Base
Golsh	RN ships three tiered bunk
IA	Immediate Action
IFOR	International Force
Jankers	Close arrest
J/T	Junior Technician
MU	Maintenance Unit
ND	Negligent Discharge from a weapon.
OCU	Operational Conversion Unit
PJI	Parachute Jump Instructor
PTSD	Post Traumatic Stress Disorder
PX	Post Exchange (US)
RPG	Rocket Propelled Grenade
R&R	Rest and Recuperation
SAC	Senior Aircraftman
SATCO	Senior Air Traffic Control Officer
SBS	Special Boat Service
Sanger	Fortified Guard Post
SEME	School of Electrical and Mechanical Engineers
SHAPE	Supreme Headquarters Allied Powers Europe
Snowball's	RAF Police - white topped SD hats.
SRIM	Service Radio Installation Modification
TACEVAL	Tactical Evaluation
Train Smash	Tinned Tomatoes (Naval slang)
WRAF	Women's Royal Air Force